Samba
Pocket Reference

SECOND EDITION

Samba
Pocket Reference

*Jay Ts, Robert Eckstein,
and David Collier-Brown*

O'REILLY®

Beijing · Cambridge · Farnham · Köln · Paris · Sebastopol · Taipei · Tokyo

Samba Pocket Reference, Second Edition

by Jay Ts, Robert Eckstein, and David Collier-Brown

Copyright © 2003, 2001 O'Reilly & Associates, Inc. All rights reserved.
Printed in the United States of America.

Published by O'Reilly & Associates, Inc., 1005 Gravenstein Highway North,
Sebastopol, CA 95472.

O'Reilly & Associates books may be purchased for educational,
business, or sales promotional use. Online editions are also available
for most titles (*safari.oreilly.com*). For more information, contact our
corporate/institutional sales department: (800) 998-9938 or
corporate@oreilly.com.

Editor:	Andy Oram
Production Editor:	Philip Dangler
Cover Designer:	Ellie Volckhausen
Interior Designer:	David Futato

Printing History:

April 2001:	First Edition.
April 2003:	Second Edition.

This updated and revised edition is based on material from O'Reilly's
Using Samba.

0-596-00546-6
[C]

Contents

Samba Pocket Reference

Introduction

Samba is an extremely useful networking tool for anyone who has both Windows and Unix systems on a network. When run on a Unix system (including Linux, BSD, or Mac OS X), Samba allows Windows to access files and printers shared by the Unix host, and permits Unix users to access resources shared by Windows systems.

This pocket reference, which is based on *Using Samba* (O'Reilly), summarizes the many commands and tools available to Samba administrators. It provides examples of proper command syntax and can help you choose the best configuration options for your network.

WARNING

This book does not include enough information for an inexperienced Samba administrator. Running Samba entails operational and security concerns, and its options have subtle interactions and side effects. Even if you are starting from an example or existing configuration file, please study *Using Samba* or another introductory book before trying to administer Samba.

A Samba server offers the following services:

- Share one or more directory trees
- Share one or more Distributed filesystem (Dfs) trees

- Share printers installed on the server among Windows clients on the network
- Assist clients with network browsing
- Authenticate clients logging onto a Windows domain
- Provide or assist with Windows Internet Name Service (WINS) name-server resolution

The Samba suite also includes client tools that allow users on a Unix system to access folders and printers offered by networked Windows systems and Samba servers.

Contents

"Configuration File Options" lists the types of lines you can put in your Samba configuration file, usually named *smb.conf*.

"Samba Daemons" lists command-line options and related information for running the Samba daemons. "Samba Distribution Programs" lists various commands included in the Samba distribution that you can run from the Unix shell on the system hosting Samba.

"Example Configuration Files" shows how the configuration options fit together in typical environments. Use these as guides; do not copy them blindly.

Font Conventions

The following font conventions are followed throughout this book:

Italic
> Used for filenames, file extensions, URLs, executable files, commands, Samba daemons, and emphasis

`Constant width`
> Used to indicate Samba configuration options, code that appears in the text, variables, and command-line information that should be typed verbatim on the screen

Constant width bold

Used for commands that are entered by the user, and new configuration options that we wish to bring to readers' attention

Constant width italic

Used to indicate replaceable content in code and command-line information

[]

Used to indicate optional elements in code

Configuration File Options

This section lists each option that can be used in a Samba configuration file, which is usually named *smb.conf*. Most configuration files contain a global section of options that apply to all services (shares) and separate sections for various individual shares. If an option applies only to the global section, [global] appears to the right of its name in the following reference section.

Except where noted, when specifying elements of a list, the elements can be separated by spaces, tabs, commas, semicolons, escaped newlines, or escaped carriage returns.

Following this reference section is a glossary of value types, and a list of variables Samba recognizes.

abort shutdown script = command [global]

Allowable values: command   **Default:** (null)

Specifies a command that stops the shutdown procedure started by shutdown script. The command will be run with the UID of the connected user. New in Samba 3.0.

add machine script = command [global]

Allowable values: command   **Default:** (null)

Specifies a command that adds a computer to the Samba server's domain. New in Samba 3.0.

add printer command = command [global]

Allowable values: command   **Default:** (null)

Specifies a command that creates a new printer on the system hosting the Samba server. This command runs as root when the Windows NT/2000/XP Add Printer Wizard is run. The command will be passed a printer name, share name, port name, driver name, Windows NT/2000/XP driver location, and Windows 95/98/Me driver location, in that order. It will need to add the printer to the system and a share definition for the printer to *smb.conf*. See also add printer wizard, printing, and show add printer wizard.

add share command = command [global]

Allowable values: command   **Default:** (null)

Specifies a command that creates a new share on the Samba server. This command runs as root when a share is created using the Windows NT/2000/XP Server Manager. The client user must be logged on as the root user. The command will be passed the name of the Samba configuration file, the name of the share to be created, the full pathname of a directory on the Samba server (which must already exist), and a string to use as a comment for the share, in that order. The command must add a share definition for the share to *smb.conf*. See also add printer command, for adding a print share.

add user script = command [global]

Allowable values: command   **Default:** (null)

Specifies a command that creates a new user on the system hosting the Samba server. This command runs as root when access to a Samba share is attempted by a Windows user who does not have an account on the hosting system, but does have an account maintained by a primary domain controller on a different system. The command should accept the name of the user as a single argument that matches the behavior of typical *adduser* commands. Samba honors the %u value (username) as the argument to the command. Requires security = server or security = domain. See also delete user script.

admin users = user list

Allowable values: user list   **Default:** (null)

Specifies users who will be granted root permissions on the share by Samba.

ads server = value   [global]

Allowable values: DNS hostname or IP address   **Default:** (null)

Specifies the Active Directory server, used by Samba 3.0 for authenticating clients. Requires security = ads. New in Samba 3.0.

algorithmic rid base = number   [global]

Allowable values: positive integer   **Default:** 1000

Specifies the base value that Samba uses when calculating Windows domain realtive identifier (RID) equivalents to Unix UIDs. See also non unix account range. New in Samba 3.0.

allow hosts = host list

Allowable values: list of hosts or networks   **Default:** (null)

Specifies systems that can connect to the share or shares. If null, any system can access the share unless there is a hosts deny option. Synonym for hosts allow.

allow trusted domains = boolean   [global]

Allowable values: YES, NO   **Default:** YES

Allows access to users who lack accounts on the Samba server but have accounts in another, trusted domain. Requires security = server or security = domain.

announce as = value

[global]

Allowable values: NT, Win95, WfW   **Default:** NT

Instructs Samba to announce itself as something other than an NT server. Discouraged because it interferes with serving browse lists.

announce version = value

[global]

Allowable values: two numbers separated by a dot character   **Default:** 4.5

Instructs Samba to announce itself as a different version SMB server. Discouraged.

auth methods = list

[global]

Allowable values: guest, sam, ntdomain   **Default:** (null)

Specifies what methods Samba tries in turn to authenticate users. New in Samba 3.0.

auto services = service list

[global]

Allowable values: service list   **Default:** (null)

Specifies a list of shares that always appear in browse lists. Also called preload.

available = boolean

Allowable values: YES, NO   **Default:** YES

If set to NO, denies access to a share. The share appears in the browse list, but attempts to access it will fail.

bind interfaces only = boolean

[global]

Allowable values: YES, NO   **Default:** NO

If set to YES, shares and browsing are provided only on interfaces in an interfaces list (see interfaces). If you set this option to YES, be sure to add 127.0.0.1 to the interfaces list to allow *smbpasswd* to connect to the local system to change passwords. This is a convenience option; it does not improve security.

block size = number

Allowable values: integer   **Default:** 1024

Sets the size of disk blocks as reported by *smbd* to the client. Obsolete starting with Samba 3.0.

blocking locks = boolean

Allowable values: YES, NO   **Default:** YES

If YES, honors byte range lock requests with time limits. Samba will queue the requests and retry them until the time period expires.

browsable = boolean

Allowable values: YES, NO   **Default:** YES

Allows a share to be announced in browse lists. Also called browseable.

browse list = boolean   [global]

Allowable values: YES, NO   **Default:** YES

If YES, serves the browse list to other systems on the network. Avoid changing.

browseable = boolean

Allowable values: YES, NO   **Default:** YES

Synonym for browsable.

case sensitive = boolean   [global]

Allowable values: YES, NO   **Default:** NO

If YES, uses the exact case the client supplied when trying to resolve a filename. If NO, matches either upper- or lowercase name. Avoid changing. Also called casesignames.

casesignames = boolean   [global]

Allowable values: YES, NO   **Default:** NO

Synonym for case sensitive.

change notify timeout = number [global]

Allowable values: positive number **Default:** 60

Sets the number of seconds between checks when a client asks for notification of changes in a directory. Avoid lowering.

change share command = command [global]

Allowable values: command **Default:** (null)

Specifies a command that modifies a share definition on the Samba server. This command runs as root when a share is created using the Windows NT/2000/XP Server Manager. The client user must be logged on as the root user. The command is passed the name of the Samba configuration file, the name of the share to be modified, the full pathname of a directory on the Samba server (which must already exist), and a string to use as a comment for the share, in that order. The command modifies the share definition for the share in *smb.conf*. See also add share command and delete share command.

character set = name

Allowable values: ISO8859-1, ISO8859-2, ISO8859-5, KOI8-R **Default:** (null)

If set, translates from DOS code pages to the Western European (ISO8859-1), Eastern European (ISO8859-2), Russian Cyrillic (ISO8859-5), or Alternate Russian (KOI8-R) character set. The client code page option must be set to 850. Obsolete starting with Samba 3.0.

client code page = name

Allowable values: 437, 737, 850, 852, 861, **Default:** 850 (MS-DOS Latin 1)
866, 932, 936, 949, 950

Sets the DOS code page explicitly, overriding any previous valid chars settings. Examples of values are 850 for Western European, 437 for the U.S. standard, and 932 for Japanese Shift-JIS. Obsolete starting with Samba 3.0.

code page directory = directory [global]

Allowable values: full directory name
Default: /usr/local/samba/lib/codepages

Specifies the directory that stores code pages. Obsolete starting with Samba 3.0.

coding system = value [global]

Allowable values: euc, cap, hex, hexN, sjis, j8bb, j8bj, jis8, **Default:** (null)
j8bh, j8@b, j8@j, j8@h, j7bb, j7bj, jis7,
j7bh, j7@b, j7@j, j7@h, jubb, jubj, junet,
jubh, ju@b, ju@j, ju@h

Sets the coding system used, notably for Kanji. This is employed for filenames and should correspond to the code page in use. The client code page option must be set to 932 (Japanese Shift-JIS). Obsolete starting with Samba 3.0.

comment = string

Allowable values: string **Default:** (null)

Sets the comment corresponding to a share. The comment appears in places such as a *net view* listing or through the Network Neighborhood. See also the server string configuration option.

config file = filename [global]

Allowable values: filename **Default:** (null)

Selects a new Samba configuration file to read instead of the current one. Used to relocate the configuration file or used with % variables to select custom configuration files for some users or systems.

copy = section name

Allowable values: existing section's name **Default:** (null)

Copies the configuration of an already defined share into the share in which this option appears. Used with % variables to select custom configurations for systems, architectures, and users. Each option specified or copied takes precedence over earlier specifications of the option.

create mask = value

Allowable values: octal value from 0 to 0777   **Default:** 0744

Sets the maximum allowable permissions for new files (e.g., 0755). See also directory mask. To require certain permissions to be set, see force create mask and force directory mask. Also called create mode.

create mode = value

Allowable values: octal value from 0 to 0777   **Default:** 0744

Synonym for create mask.

csc policy = value

Allowable values: manual, documents, programs, or disable   **Default:** manual

Sets the client-side caching policy, telling them how to cache files offline if they are capable of doing so.

deadtime = number   [global]

Allowable values: number   **Default:** 0

Specifies the time in minutes before an unused connection will be terminated. Zero means never. Used to keep clients from tying up server resources for long periods of time. If used, clients must autoreconnect after the specified period of inactivity. See also keepalive.

debug hires timestamp = boolean   [global]

Allowable values: YES, NO   **Default:** NO

Changes the timestamps in log entries from seconds to microseconds. Useful for measuring performance.

debug pid = boolean   [global]

Allowable values: YES, NO   **Default:** NO

Adds the process ID of the Samba server to log lines, making it easier to debug a particular server. Requires debug timestamp = yes to work.

debug timestamp = boolean [global]

Allowable values: YES, NO **Default:** YES

Timestamps all log messages. Can be turned off when it's not useful (e.g., in debugging). Also called `timestamp logs`.

debug uid = boolean [global]

Allowable values: YES, NO **Default:** NO

Adds the real and effective user ID and group ID of the user being served to the logs, making it easier to debug one particular user.

debuglevel = number [global]

Allowable values: number **Default:** 0

Sets the logging level used. Values of 3 or more slow Samba noticeably. Also called `log level`. Recommended value is 1.

default = service name [global]

Allowable values: share name **Default:** (null)

Specifies the name of a service (share) to provide if someone requests a service he doesn't have permission to use or that doesn't exist. The path is set from the name the client specified, with any underscore (_) characters changed to slash (/) characters, allowing access to any directory on the Samba server. Use is discouraged. See also `load printers`. Also called `default service`.

default case = value

Allowable values: LOWER, UPPER **Default:** LOWER

Sets the case in which to store new filenames. LOWER indicates lowercase, and UPPER indicates uppercase.

default devmode = boolean

Allowable values: YES, NO **Default:** NO

Used with printer shares being accessed by Windows NT/2000/XP clients to set a default device mode for the printer. Can be problematic. Use with care.

default service = share name [global]

Allowable values: share name   **Default:** (null)

Synonym for default.

delete printer command = command [global]

Allowable values: command   **Default:** (null)

Specifies a command that removes a printer from the system hosting the Samba server and deletes its service definition from *smb.conf*. The command is passed a printer name as its only argument. See also add printer command, printing, and show add printer wizard.

delete readonly = boolean

Allowable values: NO, YES   **Default:** NO

If set to YES, allows delete requests to remove read-only files. This is not allowed in MS-DOS/Windows, but it is normal in Unix, which has separate directory permissions. Used with programs such as RCS.

delete share command = command

Allowable values: command   **Default:** (null)

Specifies a command that deletes a share from the Samba server. The command runs when a user logged in as the root user on a Windows NT/2000/XP system deletes a share using Server Manager. The command is passed the name of the Samba configuration file and the name of the share to be deleted. The command must remove the definition of the share from the configuration file. See also add share command and change share command.

delete user script = command [global]

Allowable values: full path to script   **Default:** (null)

Sets the command to run as root when a user connects who no longer has an account on the domain's PDC. Honors %u. Can be used to delete the user account automatically from the Samba server's host. Requires security = domain or security = user. Use with caution. See also add user script.

delete veto files = boolean

Allowable values: NO, YES   **Default:** NO

If set to YES, allows delete requests for a directory containing files or subdirectories the user can't see due to the veto files option. If set to NO, delete requests are denied and invisible files are not removed from the directory.

deny hosts = host list

Allowable values: hosts or networks   **Default:** (null)

Specifies a list of systems from which to refuse connections. Also called hosts deny.

dfree command = command   [global]

Allowable values: command   **Default:** (varies)

Specifies a command to run on the server to return free disk space. Not needed unless the Samba host system's *dfree* command does not work properly.

directory = directory

Allowable values: Unix directory name   **Default:** (varies)

Sets the path to the directory provided by a file share or used by a printer share. If the option is omitted in the [homes] share, it is set automatically to the user's home directory; otherwise, it defaults to */tmp*. For a printer share, the directory is used to spool printer files. Honors the %u (user) and %m (machine) variables. Synonym for path.

directory mask = value

Allowable values: octal value from 0 to 0777   **Default:** 0755

Sets the maximum allowable permissions for newly created directories. To require that certain permissions be set, see the force create mask and force directory mask options. Also called directory mode.

directory mode = value

Allowable values: octal value from 0 to 0777   **Default:** 0755

Synonym for directory mask.

directory security mask = value

Allowable values: octal value from 0 to 0777   **Default:** same as directory mode

Controls which permission bits can be changed if a user edits the Unix permissions of directories on the Samba server from a Windows system. Any bit that is set in the mask can be changed by the user; any bit that is clear remains the same on the directory even if the user tries to change it. Requires nt acl support = YES.

disable spools = boolean   [global]

Allowable values: YES, NO   **Default:** NO

If set to YES, Windows NT/2000/XP systems will downgrade to Lanman-style printing. Prevents printer driver uploading and downloading from working. Use with care. See also use client driver.

dns proxy = boolean   [global]

Allowable values: YES, NO   **Default:** YES

If set to YES and if wins server = YES, looks up hostnames in DNS when they are not found using WINS.

domain admin group = user list   [global]

Allowable values: usernames and/or group names   **Default:** (null)

Specifies users who are in the Domain Admins group and have domain administrator authority when Samba is the PDC. See also domain guest group and domain logons. Useful in Samba 2.2 only. Obsolete in Samba 3.0.

domain guest group = user/group list   [global]

Allowable values: list of usernames and/or group names   **Default:** (null)

Specifies users who are in the Domain Guest group when Samba is the PDC. See also domain admin group and domain logons. Useful in Samba 2.2 only. Obsolete in Samba 3.0.

domain logons = boolean
[global]

Allowable values: YES, NO **Default:** NO

Causes Samba to serve domain logons. This is one of the basic functions required when Samba is acting as the PDC.

domain master = boolean
[global]

Allowable values: YES, NO **Default:** (automatic)

Makes Samba a domain master browser for its domain. When domain logons are enabled, domain master defaults to YES. Otherwise, it defaults to NO.

dont descend = list

Allowable values: list of directories **Default:** (null)

Prohibits a change directory or search in the directories specified. This is a browsing-convenience option; it doesn't provide any extra security.

dos filemode = boolean

Allowable values: YES, NO **Default:** NO

Allows anyone with write permissions to change permissions on a file, as allowed by MS-DOS.

dos filetime resolution = boolean

Allowable values: YES, NO **Default:** NO

Sets file times on Unix to match MS-DOS standards (rounding to the next even second). Recommended if using Visual C++ or a PC *make* program to avoid remaking the programs unnecessarily. Use with the dos filetimes option.

dos filetimes = boolean

Allowable values: YES, NO **Default:** NO

Allows nonowners to change file times if they can write to the files, matching the behavior of MS-DOS and Windows. See also dos filetime resolution.

encrypt passwords = boolean [global]

Allowable values: YES, NO   **Default:** NO in Samba 2.2, YES in Samba 3.0

If enabled, Samba will use password encryption. Requires an *smbpasswd* file on the Samba server.

enhanced browsing = boolean [global]

Allowable values: YES, NO   **Default:** YES

Automatically synchronizes browse lists with all domain master browsers known to the WINS server. Makes cross-subnet browsing more reliable, but also can cause empty workgroups to persist forever in browse lists.

enumports command = command [global]

Allowable values: command   **Default:** (null)

Allows for a command to provide clients with customized MS-DOS/Windows port names (e.g., PRN:) corresponding to printers. Samba's default behavior is to return `Samba Printer Port`. The command must return a series of lines, with one port name per line.

exec = command

Allowable values: command   **Default:** (null)

Sets a command to run as the user before connecting to the share. All % variable substitutions can be used. Synonym for preexec. See also the postexec, root preexec, and root postexec options.

fake directory create times = boolean

Allowable values: YES, NO   **Default:** NO

A bug fix for users of Microsoft *nmake*. If YES, Samba sets directory create times such that *nmake* won't remake all files every time.

fake oplocks = boolean

Allowable values: YES, NO   **Default:** NO

If set, returns YES whenever a client asks if it can lock a file and cache it locally but does not enforce the lock on the server. Results in performance improvement for read-only shares. *Never use with read/write shares!* See also oplocks and veto oplock files.

follow symlinks = boolean

Allowable values: YES, NO   **Default:** YES

If set to YES, Samba follows symlinks in a file share(s). See the wide links option if you want to restrict symlinks to just the current share.

force create mode = value

Allowable values: octal value from 0 to 0777   **Default:** 0

Takes effect when a user on a Windows client creates a file that resides on the Samba server. This option ensures that bits set in this mask will always be set on the new file. Used with the create mask configuration option.

force directory mode = value

Allowable values: octal value from 0 to 0777   **Default:** 0

Takes effect when a user on a Windows client creates a directory on the Samba server. This option ensures that bits set in the mask will be set on every newly created directory. Used with directory mask.

force directory security mode = value

Allowable values: octal value from 0 to 0777
Default: same as force directory mode

Takes effect when a user on a Windows client edits the Unix permissions of a directory on the Samba server. This option ensures that bits set in this mask will be set on the directory. Requires nt acl support = YES.

force group = value

Allowable values: a Unix group name   **Default:** (null)

Sets the effective group name assigned to all users accessing a share. Used to override a user's normal group memberships.

force security mode = value

Allowable values: octal value from 0 to 0777   **Default:** same as force create mode

Takes effect when a user on a Windows client edits the Unix permissions of a file on the Samba server. This option ensures that bits set in the mask will always be set on the file. Requires nt acl support = YES. See also force directory security mode for directories.

force unknown acl user = boolean

Allowable values: YES, NO   **Default:** NO

When set, unknown users or groups in Windows NT ACLs will be mapped to the user or group of the connected user. Obsolete starting with Samba 3.0.

force user = value

Allowable values: a single username   **Default:** (null)

Sets the effective username assigned to all users accessing a share. Discouraged.

fstype = string

Allowable values: NTFS, FAT, Samba   **Default:** NTFS

Sets the filesystem type reported to the client. Avoid changing.

getwd cache = boolean

[global]

Allowable values: YES, NO   **Default:** YES

Caches the current directory for performance. Recommended with the wide links option.

group = value

Allowable values: a Unix group name   **Default:** (null)

Synonym for force group.

guest account = value

Allowable values: a single username   **Default:** (varies)

Sets the name of the unprivileged Unix account to use for tasks such as printing and for accessing shares marked with guest ok. The default is specified at compile time and is usually set to nobody.

guest ok = boolean

Allowable values: YES, NO   **Default:** NO

If set to YES, passwords are not needed for this share. Used with security = share. Synonym for public.

guest only = boolean

Allowable values: YES, NO   **Default:** NO

Forces users of a share to log on as the guest account. Requires guest ok or public to be YES. Also called only guest.

hide dot files = boolean

Allowable values: YES, NO   **Default:** YES

Treats files with names beginning with a dot as if they had the MS-DOS hidden attribute set. The files are either not displayed on a Windows client or appear grayed-out, depending on the settings on the client.

hide files = slash-separated list

Allowable values: patterns, separated by / characters   **Default:** (null)

Specifies a list of file or directory names on which to set the MS-DOS hidden attribute. Names can contain ? or * pattern characters and % variables. See also hide dot files and veto files.

hide local users = boolean

        [global]

Allowable values: YES, NO   **Default:** NO

If set to YES, hides Unix-specific dummy accounts (root, wheel, floppy, etc.) from clients.

hide unreadable = boolean

Allowable values: YES, NO   **Default:** NO

If set to YES, hides all unreadable files.

homedir map = name   [global]

Allowable values: NIS map name   **Default:** (null)

Used with nis homedir to locate a user's Unix home directory from Sun NIS (not NIS+).

host msdfs = boolean   [global]

Allowable values: YES, NO   **Default:** NO

If set to YES and Samba was configured with the --with-msdfs option, provides Microsoft Distributed filesystem (Dfs) service, allowing Dfs-capable clients to browse Dfs trees on the Samba server. See also msdfs root.

hosts allow = host list

Allowable values: list of hosts or networks   **Default:** (null)

Specifies a list of systems that can access the share. If null, any system can access the share unless there is a hosts deny option. Synonym for allow hosts.

hosts deny = host list

Allowable values: list of hosts or networks   **Default:** (null)

Specifies a list of systems that cannot connect to the share. Synonym for deny hosts.

hosts equiv = filename   [global]

Allowable values: name of file   **Default:** (null)

Specifies the path to a file of trusted systems from which passwordless logons are allowed. Strongly discouraged because Windows NT/2000/XP users can always override the username—the only security in this scheme.

include = filename

Allowable values: name of file   **Default:** (null)

Includes the named file in *smb.conf* at the line where it appears. This option accepts most variables, but not %u (user), %P (current share's root directory), or %S (current share's name) because they are not set at the time the file is read.

inherit acls = boolean

Allowable values: YES, NO   **Default:** NO

If set, files and subdirectories are created with the same ACLs as their parent directories. Directories are given Unix permissions of 0777 (full permissions) ensuring that the ACL on the directory will govern the actual permissions given to clients. Requires POSIX ACL support to be provided on the Samba host system.

inherit permissions = boolean

Allowable values: YES, NO   **Default:** NO

If set, files and subdirectories are created with the same permissions as their parent directories. This allows Unix directory permissions to be propagated automatically to new files and subdirectories, especially in the [homes] share. This option overrides create mask, directory mask, force create mode, and force directory mode, but not map archive, map hidden, or map system. Samba never sets the setuid bit when creating a file or directory.

interfaces = interface list   [global]

Allowable values: interface list   **Default:** (null) (all interfaces except 127.0.0.1)

Sets the interfaces to which Samba will respond. The default is the system's primary interface only. Recommended on multihomed systems or to override erroneous addresses and netmasks. Allows interface names such as eth0, DNS names, address/netmask pairs, and broadcast/netmask pairs. See also bind interfaces only.

invalid users = user list

Allowable values: user list   **Default:** (null)

Specifies a list of users not permitted access to the share.

keepalive = number [global]

Allowable values: number of seconds   **Default:** 300

Sets the number of seconds between checks for a crashed client. The value of 0 causes no checks to be performed. Setting keepalive = 3600 will turn on checks every hour. A value of 600 (every 10 minutes) is recommended if you want more frequent checks. See also socket options for another approach.

kernel oplocks = boolean [global]

Allowable values: YES, NO   **Default:** YES

Breaks the oplock when a local Unix process or NFS operation accesses an oplocked file, thus preventing corruption. This works only on operating systems that support kernel-based oplocks, such as Linux 2.4 and Irix. Avoid changing. See also oplocks and level2 oplocks.

lanman auth = boolean [global]

Allowable values: YES, NO   **Default:** YES

If set to YES, allows clients to use the (weak) LANMAN password hash used by Windows 95/98/Me. If set to NO, allows only the better NT1 hash used by Windows NT/2000/XP.

large readwrite = boolean [global]

Allowable values: YES, NO   **Default:** NO in Samba 2.2, YES in Samba 3.0

If set to YES, allows Windows 2000/XP to read and write 64KB at a time to improve performance. Requires Samba to be hosted by a 64-bit OS, such as Linux 2.4, Irix, or Solaris. Somewhat experimental.

ldap admin dn = string [global]

Allowable values: Distinguished Name   **Default:** (null)

Sets the Distinguished Name used by Samba when contacting the LDAP server. Requires that Samba be configured with the --with-ldapsam configuration option. Experimental option added in Samba 2.2.3 and obsolete in Samba 3.0.

ldap filter = string [global]

Allowable values: LDAP search filter   **Default:** `(&(uid=%u)`
`(objectclass=sambaAccount))`

Sets the LDAP search filter. Requires that Samba be configured with the `--with-ldapsam` configuration option. Experimental option added in Samba 2.2.3 and obsolete in Samba 3.0.

ldap port = number [global]

Allowable values: positive integer   **Default:** In Samba 2.2, 636 if `ldap ssl = on;`
otherwise 389

Sets the TCP port number for contacting the LDAP server. Requires that Samba be configured with the `--with-ldapsam` configuration option. Experimental option added in Samba 2.2.3 and obsolete starting with Samba 3.0. See also `ldap ssl`.

ldap server = value [global]

Allowable values: fully qualified domain name   **Default:** `localhost`

Sets the domain name of the LDAP server. Requires that Samba be configured with the `--with-ldapsam` configuration option. Experimental option added in Samba 2.2.3 and obsolete starting with Samba 3.0.

ldap ssl = value [global]

Allowable values: `ON`, `OFF`, `START_TLS`   **Default:** `ON`

Sets whether Samba uses SSL to contact the LDAP server. `ON` and `OFF` turn SSL encryption on or off. The `START_TLS` setting causes Samba to use LDAPv3 StartTLS extended operation. Requires that Samba be configured with the `--with-ldapsam` configuration option. Experimental option added in Samba 2.2.3 and obsolete in Samba 3.0.

ldap suffix = string [global]

Allowable values: Distinguished Name   **Default:** (null)

Sets the base Distinguished Name to use for LDAP searches. Requires that Samba be configured with the `--with-ldapsam` configuration option. Experimental option added in Samba 2.2.3 and obsolete in Samba 3.0.

level2 oplocks = boolean

Allowable values: YES, NO **Default:** YES

Allows files to be cached read-only on the client when multiple clients have opened the file. This allows executables to be cached locally, improving performance.

lm announce = value [global]

Allowable values: AUTO, YES, NO **Default:** AUTO

Produces OS/2 SMB broadcasts at an interval specified by the lm interval option. YES/NO turns them on/off unconditionally. AUTO causes the Samba server to wait for a LAN manager announcement from another client before sending one out. Required for OS/2 client browsing.

lm interval = number [global]

Allowable values: number of seconds **Default:** 60

Sets the time period, in seconds, between OS/2 SMB broadcast announcements.

load printers = boolean [global]

Allowable values: YES, NO **Default:** YES

Loads all printer names from the system's *printcap* file into the browse list. Uses configuration options from the [printers] section.

local master = boolean [global]

Allowable values: YES, NO **Default:** YES

Allows Samba to participate in elections for the local master browser. See also domain master and os level.

lock dir = directory [global]

Allowable values: name of directory **Default:** /usr/local/samba/var/locks

Synonym for lock directory.

lock directory = directory [global]

Allowable values: name of directory   **Default:** /usr/local/samba/var/locks

Sets a directory in which to keep lock files. The directory must be writable by Samba and readable by everyone. Also called lock dir.

lock spin count = number [global]

Allowable values: positive integer   **Default:** 2

Sets the number of attempts to attain a byte range lock. See also lock spin time.

lock spin time = number [global]

Allowable values: number of microseconds   **Default:** 10

Sets the number of microseconds between attempts to attain a lock. See also lock spin count.

locking = boolean

Allowable values: YES, NO   **Default:** YES

Performs file locking. If set to NO, Samba accepts lock requests but won't actually lock resources. Turn off for read-only filesystems.

log file = filename [global]

Allowable values: name of file   **Default:** (varies)

Sets the name and location of the log file. Allows all % variables.

log level = number [global]

Allowable values: number   **Default:** 0

Sets the logging level used. Values of 3 or more slow the system noticeably. Recommended value is 1. Synonym for debug level.

logon drive = value [global]

Allowable values: MS-DOS drive name   **Default:** Z:

Sets the drive to be used as a home directory for domain logons by Windows NT/2000/XP clients. See also logon home.

logon home = directory [global]

Allowable values: UNC of shared directory   **Default:** \\%N\%U

Sets the home directory of a Windows 95/98/Me or NT/2000/XP user. Allows NET USE H:/HOME from the command prompt if Samba is acting as a logon server. Append \profile or other directory to the value of this parameter if storing Windows 95/98/Me profiles in a subdirectory of the user's home directory. See logon path for Windows NT/2000/XP roaming profiles.

logon path = directory [global]

Allowable values: UNC of shared directory   **Default:** \\%N\%U\profile

Sets the path to the directory where Windows NT/2000/XP roaming profiles are stored. See also logon home for Windows 95/98/Me roaming profiles.

logon script = directory [global]

Allowable values: UNC of shared file   **Default:** (null)

Sets the pathname (relative to the [netlogon] share) of an MS-DOS/NT command to run on the client at logon time. Allows all % variables.

lppause command = command

Allowable values: command   **Default:** (varies)

Sets the command to pause a print job. Honors the %p (printer name) and %j (job number) variables.

lpq cache time = number [global]

Allowable values: number of seconds   **Default:** 10

Sets how long to keep print queue status cached, in seconds.

lpq command = command

Allowable values: command   **Default:** (varies)

Sets the command used to get printer status. Usually initialized to a default value by the printing option. Honors the %p (printer name) variable.

lpresume command = command

Allowable values: command   **Default:** (varies)

Sets the command to resume a paused print job. Honors the %p (printer name) and %j (job number) variables.

lprm command = command

Allowable values: command   **Default:** (varies)

Sets the command to delete a print job. Usually initialized to a default value by the printing option. Honors the %p (printer name) and %j (job number) variables.

machine password timeout = number

Allowable values: number of seconds   **Default:** 604800 (1 week)

Sets the period between (NT domain) computer account password changes.

magic output = filename

Allowable values: name of file   **Default:** command.out

Sets the output file for the magic scripts option. Default is the command name, followed by the *.out* extension.

magic script = filename

Allowable values: name of file   **Default:** (null)

Sets a filename for execution via a shell whenever the file is closed from the client, allowing clients to run commands on the server. The scripts will be deleted on completion, if permissions allow. Use is discouraged.

mangle case = boolean

Allowable values: YES, NO   **Default:** NO

Mangles a name if it is in mixed case.

mangled map = map list

Allowable values: list of to/from pairs   **Default:** (null)

Sets up a table of names to remap (e.g., *.html* to *.htm*).

mangled names = boolean

Allowable values: YES, NO   **Default:** YES

Sets Samba to abbreviate to the MS-DOS 8.3 style names that are too long or have unsupported characters.

mangled stack = number   [global]

Allowable values: number   **Default:** 50

Sets the size of the cache of recently mangled filenames.

mangling char = character

Allowable values: character   **Default:** ~

Sets the unique mangling character used in all mangled names.

mangling method = string   [global]

Allowable values: hash, hash2   **Default:** hash

Sets the algorithm used to mangle filenames. The hash2 method is a newer method introduced in Samba 2.2.x, and it creates different filenames than the hash method.

map archive = boolean

Allowable values: YES, NO   **Default:** YES

If YES, Samba sets the executable-by-user (0100) bit on Unix files if the MS-DOS archive attribute is set. If used, the create mask must contain the 0100 bit.

map hidden = boolean

Allowable values: YES, NO   **Default:** NO

If YES, Samba sets the executable-by-other (0001) bit on Unix files if the MS-DOS hidden attribute is set. If used, the create mask option must contain the 0001 bit.

map system = boolean

Allowable values: YES, NO   **Default:** NO

If YES, Samba sets the executable-by-group (0010) bit on Unix files
if the MS-DOS system attribute is set. If used, the create mask
must contain the 0010 bit.

map to guest = value   [global]

Allowable values: Never, Bad User, Bad Password   **Default:** Never

If set to Bad User, allows users without accounts on the Samba
system to log in and be assigned the guest account. This option
can be used as part of making public shares for anyone to use. If
set to Bad Password, users who mistype their passwords will be
logged in to the guest account instead of their own. Because no
warning is given, the Bad Password setting can be extremely
confusing: we recommend against it. The default setting of Never
prevents users without accounts from logging in.

max connections = number

Allowable values: number   **Default:** 0 (infinity)

Sets the maximum number of share connections allowed from
each client system.

max disk size = number   [global]

Allowable values: size in MB   **Default:** 0 (no limit)

Sets the maximum disk size/free-space size (in megabytes) to
return to the client. Some clients or applications can't understand
large maximum disk sizes.

max log size = number   [global]

Allowable values: size in KB   **Default:** 5000

Sets the size (in kilobytes) at which Samba will start a new log file.
The current log file will be renamed with a *.old* extension,
replacing any existing file with that name.

max mux = number   [global]

Allowable values: number   **Default:** 50

Sets the number of simultaneous SMB operations that Samba
clients can make. Avoid changing.

max open files = number   [global]

Allowable values: number   **Default:** 10000

Limits the number of files a Samba process will try to keep open at
one time. Samba allows you to set this to less than the maximum
imposed by the Unix host operating system. Avoid changing.

max print jobs = number

Allowable values: positive integer   **Default:** 1000

Limits the number of jobs that can be in the queue for this printer
share at any one time. The printer will report out of space if the
limit is exceeded. See also total print jobs.

max protocol = name   [global]

Allowable values: CORE, COREPLUS, LANMAN1, LANMAN2, NT1   **Default:** NT1

If set, limits the negotiation to the protocol specified, or older. See
min protocol. Avoid using.

max smbd processes = number   [global]

Allowable values: integer   **Default:** 0 (no limit)

Limits the number of users who can connect to the server. Used to
prevent degraded service under an overload, at the cost of refusing
services entirely.

max ttl = number   [global]

Allowable values: number of seconds   **Default:** 259200 (3 days)

Sets the time to live (TTL) of NetBIOS names in the *nmbd* WINS
cache. Avoid changing.

max wins ttl = number [global]

Allowable values: number of seconds   **Default:** 518400 (6 days)

Limits the TTL, in seconds, of a NetBIOS name in the *nmbd* WINS cache. Avoid changing. See also min wins ttl.

max xmit = number [global]

Allowable values: size in bytes   **Default:** 65535

Sets the maximum packet size negotiated by Samba. This is a tuning parameter for slow links and bugs in older clients. Values less than 2048 are discouraged.

message command = command [global]

Allowable values: command   **Default:** (null)

Sets the command to run on the server when a Windows Messenger Service message arrives from a client. If it does not complete quickly, the command must end in & to allow immediate return. Honors all % variables except %u (user) and supports the extra variables %s (filename the message is in), %t (destination system), and %f (from).

min passwd length = number [global]

Allowable values: integer   **Default:** 5

Synonym for min password length.

min password length = number [global]

Allowable values: integer   **Default:** 5

Sets the shortest Unix password allowed by Samba when updating a user's password on its system. Also called min passwd length.

min print space = number

Allowable values: space in kilobytes   **Default:** 0 (unlimited)

Sets the minimum spool space required before accepting a print request.

min protocol = name [global]

Allowable values: CORE, COREPLUS, LANMAN1, LANMAN2, NT1   **Default:** CORE

If set, prevents use of old (less secure) protocols. Using NT1 disables MS-DOS clients. See also `lanman auth`.

min wins ttl = number [global]

Allowable values: number of seconds   **Default:** 21600 (6 hours)

Sets the minimum TTL, in seconds, of a NetBIOS name in the *nmbd* WINS cache. Avoid changing.

msdfs root = boolean

Allowable values: YES, NO   **Default:** NO

Makes the share a Dfs root. Requires the --with-msdfs configure option. Any symbolic links of the form msdfs:*server\share* will be seen as Dfs links. See also `host msdfs`.

name resolve order = list [global]

Allowable values: lmhosts, wins, host, bcast   **Default:** lmhosts, host, wins, bcast

Sets the order of lookup when trying to get IP addresses from names. The host parameter carries out a regular name lookup using the server's normal sources: */etc/hosts*, DNS, NIS, or a combination of these.

netbios aliases = list [global]

Allowable values: list of NetBIOS names   **Default:** (null)

Adds additional NetBIOS names by which the Samba server will advertise itself.

netbios name = value

Allowable values: local hostname   **Default:** DNS name of system

Sets the NetBIOS name by which a Samba server is known, or the primary name if NetBIOS aliases exist. See also `netbios aliases`.

netbios scope = string

Allowable values: string   **Default:** (null)

Sets the NetBIOS scope string, an early predecessor of work-groups. Samba will not communicate with a system with a different scope. This option is not recommended.

nis homedir = boolean
[global]

Allowable values: YES, NO   **Default:** NO

If YES, the homedir map is used to look up the server hosting the user's home directory and return it to the client. The client will contact that system to connect to the share. This avoids mounting from a system that doesn't actually have the directory, which would cause the data to be transmitted twice. The system with the home directories must be an SMB server.

non unix account range = numeric range
[global]

Allowable values: range of positive integers   **Default:** (null)

Specifies a range of Unix UIDs for Samba to use for user accounts and computer accounts that are maintained outside of */etc/passwd*. The UIDs in this range must not overlap those of regular Unix users in */etc/passwd*. See also algorithmic rid base. New in Samba 3.0.

nt acl support = boolean

Allowable values: YES, NO   **Default:** YES

Causes the Samba server to map Unix permissions to Windows NT ACLs.

nt pipe support = boolean
[global]

Allowable values: YES, NO   **Default:** YES

Allows turning off of NT-specific pipe calls. This is a developer/benchmarking option and might be removed in the future. Avoid changing.

nt smb support = boolean [global]

Allowable values: YES, NO   **Default:** YES

If YES, allows the use of NT-specific SMBs. This is a developer/benchmarking option that is obsolete in Samba 3.0. Avoid changing.

nt status support = boolean [global]

Allowable values: YES, NO   **Default:** YES

If YES, allows the use of NT-specific status messages. This is a developer/benchmarking option and might be removed in the future. Avoid changing.

null passwords = boolean [global]

Allowable values: YES, NO   **Default:** NO

If YES, allows access to accounts that have null passwords. Strongly discouraged.

obey pam restrictions = boolean [global]

Allowable values: YES, NO   **Default:** NO

If set, Samba will adhere to the PAM's account and session restrictions. Requires --with-pam configuration option.

only guest = boolean

Allowable values: YES, NO   **Default:** NO

Forces users of a share to log on as the guest account. Synonym for guest only. Requires guest ok or public to be YES.

only user = boolean

Allowable values: YES, NO   **Default:** NO

Requires that users of the share be in the list specified by the user option.

oplock break wait time = number
[global]

Allowable values: number of milliseconds   **Default:** 0

This is an advanced tuning parameter and is recommended only for experts who know how Samba handles oplocks. This option might need to be set if a Windows system fails to release an oplock in response to a break request from the Samba server. Due to bugs on some Windows systems, they might fail to respond if Samba responds too quickly; the default on this option can be lengthened in such cases.

oplock contention limit = number

Allowable values: number   **Default:** 2

This is an advanced tuning parameter and is recommended only for experts who know how Samba handles oplocks. It causes Samba to refuse to grant an oplock if the number of clients contending for a file exceeds the specified value.

oplocks = boolean

Allowable values: YES, NO   **Default:** YES

If YES, supports local caching of oplocked files on the client. This improves performance by about 30%, but may lead to corrupted files if network hardware or client software is unreliable. See also fake oplocks and veto oplock files.

os level = number
[global]

Allowable values: integer   **Default:** 20

Sets the candidacy of the server when electing a browse master. Used with the domain master or local master options. You can set a higher value than a competing operating system if you want Samba to win. Windows for Workgroups and Windows 95/98/Me use 1. Windows NT/2000/XP, when not acting as a PDC, use 16 and, when acting as a PDC, use 32. Warning: this can override non-Samba browse masters unexpectedly.

os2 driver map = filename [global]

Allowable values: name of file **Default:** (null)

Specifies a file containing mappings of Windows NT printer driver names to OS/2 printer driver names.

pam password change = boolean [global]

Allowable values: YES, NO **Default:** NO

If YES, and if Samba is configured with --with-pam, PAM is allowed to handle password changes from clients, instead of using the program defined by the passwd program parameter.

panic action = command [global]

Allowable values: command **Default:** (null)

Sets the command to run when Samba panics. Honors all % variables. For Samba developers and testers, /usr/bin/X11/xterm -display :0 -e gdb /samba/bin/smbd %d is a possible value.

passdb backend = list [global]

Allowable values: smbpasswd, smbpasswd_nua, **Default:** smbpasswd
tdbsam, tdbsam_nua, plugin

Specifies methods Samba uses to store and retrieve passwords when using a method other than the Unix system's /etc/passwd. See also non unix account range. New in Samba 3.0.

passwd chat = string [global]

Allowable values: sequence of strings **Default:** compiled-in value

Sets the chat strings used to change passwords on the server. Supports the variables %o (old password) and %n (new password) and allows the escapes \r, \n, \t, and \s (space) in the sequence. See also unix password sync, passwd program, passwd chat debug, and pam password change.

passwd chat debug = boolean [global]

Allowable values: YES, NO   **Default:** NO

Logs an entire password chat, including passwords passed, with a
log level of 100. For debugging only. See also passwd chat, pam
password change, and passwd program.

passwd program = command [global]

Allowable values: command   **Default:** /bin/passwd

Sets the command used to change a user's password. Will be run
as root. Supports %u (user). See also unix password sync.

password level = number [global]

Allowable values: number   **Default:** 0

Specifies the number of uppercase-letter permutations used to
match passwords. A workaround for clients that change passwords to a single case before sending them to the Samba server.
Causes repeated login attempts with mixed-case passwords,
which can trigger account lockouts. Required for Windows 95/
98/Me, plain-text passwords, and mixed-case passwords. Try to
avoid using.

password server = list

Allowable values: list of NetBIOS names   **Default:** (null)

Specifies a list of SMB servers that validate passwords. Used with
a Windows NT/2000 password server (PDC or BDC) and the
security = server or security = domain configuration options.
Caution: a Windows NT/2000 password server must allow logins
from the Samba server. If set to *, Samba will look up the PDC by
resolving the NetBIOS name WORKGROUP<1C>.

path = directory

Allowable values: name of directory   **Default:** (varies)

Sets the path to the directory provided by a file share or used by a
printer share. If the option is omitted, it is set automatically in the
[homes] share to the user's home directory; otherwise, defaults to
/tmp. Honors the %u (user) and %m (machine) variables.

pid directory = directory

Allowable values: name of directory   **Default:** `/usr/local/samba/var/locks`

Sets the path to the directory where PID files are located.

posix locking = boolean

Allowable values: YES, NO   **Default:** YES

If set to YES, Samba will map file locks owned by SMB clients to POSIX locks. Avoid changing.

postexec = command

Allowable values: command   **Default:** (null)

Sets a command to run as the user after disconnecting from the share. All % variable substitutions can be used. See also the preexec, root preexec, and root postexec options.

postscript = boolean

Allowable values: YES, NO   **Default:** NO

Forces a printer to recognize a file as PostScript by inserting %! as the first line. Works only if the printer is actually PostScript-compatible.

preexec = command

Allowable values: command   **Default:** (null)

Sets a command to run as the user before connecting to the share. Synonym for exec. All % variable substitutions can be used. See also the postexec, root preexec, and root postexec options.

preexec close = boolean

Allowable values: YES, NO   **Default:** NO

If set, allows the preexec command to decide if the share can be accessed by the user. If the command returns a nonzero return code, the user is denied permission to connect.

preferred master = boolean [global]

Allowable values: YES, NO   **Default:** (automatic)

If YES, Samba is the preferred master browser. Causes Samba to call a browsing election when it comes online. See also os level.

prefered master = boolean [global]

Allowable values: YES, NO   **Default:** (automatic)

Synonym for preferred master.

preload = service list

Allowable values: list of shares   **Default:** (null)

Specifies a list of shares that always appears in browse lists. Synonym for auto services. See also load printers.

preserve case = boolean

Allowable values: YES, NO   **Default:** YES

Leaves filenames in the case sent by the client. If NO, it forces filenames to the case specified by the default case option. See also short preserve case.

printable = boolean

Allowable values: YES, NO   **Default:** NO

Sets a share to be a print share. Required for all printers. Synonym for print ok.

printcap name = filename [global]

Allowable values: name of file   **Default:** /etc/printcap

Sets the path to the printer capabilities file used by the [printers] share. The default value changes to /etc/qconfig under AIX and lpstat on System V. Also called printcap.

print command = command

Allowable values: command   **Default:** (varies)

Sets the command used to send a spooled file to the printer. Usually initialized to a default value corresponding to the printing option. This option honors the %p (printer name), %s (spool file), and %f (spool file as a relative path) variables. The command must delete the spool file.

printer = name

Allowable values: printer name   **Default:** lp

Sets the name of the Unix printer used by the share. Also called printer name.

printer admin = user list

Allowable values: user list   **Default:** (null)

Specifies users who can administer a printer using the remote printer administration interface on a Windows system. The root user always has these privileges.

printer driver = name

Allowable values: exact printer driver string used by Windows   **Default:** (null)

Sets the string to pass to Windows when asked which driver to use to prepare files for a printer share. Note that the value is case-sensitive. Part of pre-2.2 printing system. Deprecated.

printer driver file = filename   [global]

Allowable values: name of file
Default: /usr/local/samba/printers/printers.def

Sets the location of a *msprint.def* file. Usable by Windows 95/98/ Me. Part of pre-2.2 printing system. Deprecated.

printer driver location = directory

Allowable values: UNC of shared directory   **Default:** \\server\PRINTER$

Sets the location of the driver for a particular printer. The value is the pathname of the share that stores the printer driver files. Part of pre-2.2 printing system. Deprecated.

printer name = name

Allowable values: name   **Default:** (null)

Synonym for printer.

printing = value

Allowable values: bsd, sysv, hpux, aix, qnx,   **Default:** bsd
            plp, softq, lprng, cups

Sets the printing style to a value other than the one compiled into the executable. This sets initial values of at least print command, lpq command, and lprm command.

print ok = boolean

Allowable values: YES, NO   **Default:** NO

Synonym for printable.

private directory = directory   [global]

Allowable values: name of directory   **Default:** /usr/local/samba/private

Specifies the directory used for storing security-sensitive files such as *smbpasswd* and *secrets.tdb*. New in Samba 3.0.

protocol = name   [global]

Allowable values: NT1, LANMAN2, LANMAN1, COREPLUS, CORE   **Default:** NT1

Synonym for max protocol.

public = boolean

Allowable values: YES, NO   **Default:** NO

If YES, passwords are not needed for this share. Also called guest ok.

queuepause command = command

Allowable values: full path to script   **Default:** (varies)

Sets the command used to pause a print queue. Usually initialized to a default value by the printing option.

queueresume command = command

Allowable values: full path to script   **Default:** (varies)

Sets the command used to resume a print queue. Usually initialized to a default value by the printing option.

read bmpx = boolean

Allowable values: YES, NO   **Default:** NO

If set to YES, supports the "Read Block Multiplex" message. Avoid changing.

read list = list

Allowable values: list of user and/or group names   **Default:** (null)

Specifies a list of users given read-only access to a writable share.

read only = boolean

Allowable values: YES, NO   **Default:** NO

Sets a share to read-only. Antonym of `writable`, `writeable`, and `write ok`.

read raw = boolean   [global]

Allowable values: YES, NO   **Default:** YES

Allows clients to read data using a 64K packet size. Recommended.

read size = number   [global]

Allowable values: positive integer   **Default:** 16384

Allows disk reads and writes to overlap network reads and writes. A tuning parameter. Do not set larger than the default.

realm = string   [global]

Allowable values: Kerberos realm name   **Default:** (null)

Specifies the realm name for Kerberos 5 authentication. Requires the `--with-krb5` configure option. New in Samba 3.0.

remote announce = remote list   [global]

Allowable values: list of remote addresses   **Default:** (null)

Adds workgroups to the list on which the Samba server will announce itself. Specified as an IP address and optional workgroup (for instance, `192.168.220.215/SIMPLE`) with multiple entries separated by spaces. Addresses can be the specific address of the browse master on a subnet or on directed broadcasts (i.e., ###.###.###.255). The server will appear on those workgroups' browse lists. Does not require WINS.

remote browse sync = list [global]

Allowable values: IP addresses   **Default:** (null)

Perform browse list synchronization with other Samba local master browsers. Addresses can be specific addresses or directed broadcasts (i.e., ###.###.###.255). The latter causes Samba to locate the local master browser on that subnet.

restrict anonymous = boolean [global]

Allowable values: YES, NO   **Default:** NO

Denies access to users who do not supply a username. This is disabled by default because when the Samba server acts as the domain's PDC, the option can keep a client from revalidating its computer account when someone new logs in. Use of the option is recommended only when all clients are Windows NT/2000/XP systems.

root = directory [global]

Allowable values: name of directory   **Default:** (null)

Synonym for root directory.

root dir = directory [global]

Allowable values: name of directory   **Default:** (null)

Synonym for root directory.

root directory = directory [global]

Allowable values: name of directory   **Default:** /

Specifies a directory to *chroot()* before starting daemons. Prevents any access outside that directory tree. See also the wide links configuration option. Also called root and root dir.

root postexec = command

Allowable values: command   **Default:** (null)

Sets a command to run as root after disconnecting from the share. All % variable substitutions can be used. See also the preexec, postexec, and root preexec configuration options. Runs after the user's postexec command. Use with caution.

root preexec = command

Allowable values: command   **Default:** (null)

Sets a command to run as root before connecting to the share. All % variable substitutions can be used. See also the preexec, postexec, and root postexec configuration options. Runs before the user's preexec command. Use with caution.

root preexec close = boolean

Allowable values: YES, NO   **Default:** NO

If set, allows the root preexec command to decide if the share can be accessed by the user. If the command returns a nonzero return code, the user will be denied permission to connect. All % variable substitutions can be used.

security = value   [global]

Allowable values: share, user, server, domain, ads   **Default:** user

Sets the client authentication method. If security = share, services are password-protected, available to everyone who knows the password. If security = user, users have accounts and passwords, and are required to authenticate with the server before accessing services. If security = server, users have accounts and passwords as with security = user, and a separate system authenticates them for Samba. If security = domain, Windows NT domain authentication is implemented using a Windows NT/2000 or other Samba server to validate accounts. If security = ads, authentication is performed by Windows 2000 Active Directory. See also the password server and encrypted passwords configuration options.

security mask = value

Allowable values: octal value from 0 to 0777   **Default:** 0777

Controls which permission bits can be changed if a user on a Windows NT/2000/XP system edits the Unix permissions of files on the Samba server using the Windows system's ACL editing dialog box. Any bit that is set in the mask can be changed by the user; any bit that is clear remains the same on the file even if the user tries to change it. Requires nt acl support = YES. Note that some rarely used bits map to the DOS system, hidden, and archive bits in the file attributes in a nonintuitive way.

server string = string   [global]

Allowable values: string   **Default:** Samba %v

Sets the name that corresponds to the Samba server in browse lists. Honors the %v (Samba version number) and %h (hostname) variables.

set directory = boolean

Allowable values: YES, NO   **Default:** NO

Allows the DEC Pathworks client to use the *set dir* command.

share modes = boolean

Allowable values: YES, NO   **Default:** YES

Directs Samba to support Windows-style whole-file (deny mode) locks. Do not change.

short preserve case = boolean

Allowable values: YES, NO   **Default:** YES

If set to YES, leaves mangled 8.3-style filenames in the case sent by the client. If NO, forces the case to that specified by the default case option. See also preserve case.

show add printer wizard = boolean [global]

Allowable values: YES, NO **Default:** YES

If set, tells clients that the Add Printer Wizard can be used to add a Samba printer from Windows NT/2000/XP clients. See also add printer command, delete printer comamnd, and printer admin.

shutdown script = command [global]

Allowable values: command **Default:** (null)

Specifies a command that initiates a system shutdown. The command is run with the UID of the connected user. The %m (message), %t (delay time), %r (reboot), and %f (force) options are supported. See also abort shutdown script. New in Samba 3.0.

smb passwd file = filename [global]

Allowable values: name of file
Default: /usr/local/samba/private/smbpasswd

Overrides the compiled-in path to the encrypted password file. See also encrypted passwords and private dir.

socket address = value [global]

Allowable values: IP address **Default:** (null)

Sets the address on which to listen for connections. Default is to listen to all addresses.

socket options = list [global]

Allowable values: socket option list **Default:** TCP_NODELAY

Sets OS-specific socket options. SO_KEEPALIVE makes TCP check clients every four hours to see if they are still accessible. TCP_NODELAY sends even tiny packets to keep delay low. Both are recommended wherever the operating system supports them.

source environment = filename [global]

Allowable values: name of file **Default:** (null)

Causes Samba to read a list of environment variables from a file upon startup. This can be useful when setting up Samba in a clustered environment. The filename can begin with a "|" (pipe)

character, in which case it causes Samba to run the file as a command to obtain the variables.

The file must be owned by root and must not be world-writable. If the filename begins with a "|" character, it must point to a command that is neither world-writable nor resides in a world-writable directory.

The data should be in the form of lines such as SAMBA_NETBIOS_ NAME=*myhostname*. This value will then be available in the *smb.conf* files as %$(SAMBA_NETBIOS_NAME).

ssl = boolean [global]

Allowable values: YES, NO   **Default:** NO

Makes Samba use SSL for data exchange with some or all hosts. Requires --with-ssl configure option. Obsolete starting with Samba 3.0.

ssl CA certDir = directory [global]

Allowable values: name of directory   **Default:** /usr/local/ssl/certs

Specifies a directory containing a file for each Certification Authority (CA) that the Samba server trusts so that Samba can verify client certificates. Part of SSL support. Requires --with-ssl configure option. Obsolete starting with Samba 3.0.

ssl CA certFile = filename [global]

Allowable values: name of file
Default: /usr/local/ssl/certs/trustedCAs.pem

Specifies a file that contains information for each CA that the Samba server trusts so that Samba can verify client certificates. Part of SSL support. Requires --with-ssl configure option. Obsolete starting with Samba 3.0.

ssl ciphers = list [global]

Allowable values: list of ciphers   **Default:** (null)

Specifies which ciphers should be offered during SSL negotiation. Not recommended. Requires --with-ssl configure option. Obsolete starting with Samba 3.0.

ssl client cert = filename

Allowable values: name of file
Default: /usr/local/ssl/certs/smbclient.pem

Specifies a file containing the server's SSL certificate, for use by *smbclient* if certificates are required in this environment. Requires --with-ssl configure option. Obsolete starting with Samba 3.0.

ssl client key = filename
[global]

Allowable values: name of file
Default: /usr/local/ssl/private/smbclient.pem

Specifies a file containing the server's private SSL key, for use by *smbclient*. Requires --with-ssl configure option. Obsolete starting with Samba 3.0.

ssl compatibility = boolean
[global]

Allowable values: YES, NO   **Default:** NO

Determines whether SSLeay should be configured for bug compatibility with other SSL implementations. Not recommended. Requires --with-ssl configure option. Obsolete starting with Samba 3.0.

ssl hosts = host list
[global]

Allowable values: list of hosts or networks   **Default:** (null)

Requires that SSL be used with the hosts listed. By default, if the ssl option is set, the server requires SSL with all hosts. Requires --with-ssl configure option. Obsolete starting with Samba 3.0.

ssl hosts resign = host list
[global]

Allowable values: list of hosts or networks   **Default:** (null)

Suppresses the use of SSL with the hosts listed. By default, if the ssl option is set, the server requires SSL with all hosts. Requires --with-ssl configure option. Obsolete starting with Samba 3.0.

ssl require clientcert = boolean [global]

Allowable values: YES, NO **Default:** NO

Requires clients to use certificates when SSL is in use. This option is recommended if SSL is used. Requires --with-ssl configure option. Obsolete starting with Samba 3.0.

ssl require servercert = boolean [global]

Allowable values: YES, NO **Default:** NO

When SSL is in use, *smbclient* requires servers to use certificates. This option is recommended if SSL is used. Requires --with-ssl configure option. Obsolete starting with Samba 3.0.

ssl server cert = filename [global]

Allowable values: name of file **Default:** (null)

Specifies a file containing the server's SSL certificate. Requires --with-ssl configure option. Obsolete starting with Samba 3.0.

ssl server key = filename [global]

Allowable values: name of file **Default:** (null)

Specifies a file containing the server's private SSL key. If no file is specified and SSL is in use, the server looks up its key in its server certificate. Requires --with-ssl configure option. Obsolete starting with Samba 3.0.

ssl version = string [global]

Allowable values: ssl2, ssl3, ssl2or3, tls1 **Default:** ssl2or3

Defines which versions of the SSL protocol the server can use: Version 2 only (ssl2), Version 3 only (ssl3), Version 2 or 3 dynamically negotiated (ssl2or3), or Transport Layer Security (tls1). Requires --with-ssl configure option. Obsolete starting with Samba 3.0.

stat cache = boolean [global]

Allowable values: YES, NO **Default:** YES

Makes the Samba server cache client names for faster resolution. Should not be changed.

stat cache size = number [global]

Allowable values: number   **Default:** 50

Determines the number of client names cached for faster resolution. Should not be changed.

status = boolean [global]

Allowable values: YES, NO   **Default:** YES

If set to YES, logs connections to a file (or shared memory) accessible to *smbstatus*. Obsolete starting with Samba 3.0.

strict allocate = boolean

Allowable values: YES, NO   **Default:** NO

If set to YES, allocates all disk blocks when creating or extending the size of files, instead of using the normal sparse file allocation used on Unix. This slows the server, but results in behavior that matches that of Windows and helps Samba correctly report "out of quota" messages.

strict locking = boolean

Allowable values: YES, NO   **Default:** NO

If set to YES, checks locks on every access, not just on demand and at open time. Not recommended.

strict sync = boolean

Allowable values: YES, NO   **Default:** NO

If set to YES, Samba synchronizes to disk whenever the client sets the sync bit in a packet. If set to NO, Samba flushes data to disk whenever buffers fill. Defaults to NO because Windows 98 Explorer sets the bit (incorrectly) in all packets.

strip dot = boolean [global]

Allowable values: YES, NO   **Default:** NO

Removes trailing dots from filenames. Dysfunctional in Samba 2.2; use mangled map instead.

sync always = boolean

Allowable values: YES, NO   **Default:** NO

If set to YES, Samba forces the data to disk through *fsync*(3) after every write. Avoid except to debug crashing servers.

syslog = number   **[global]**

Allowable values: number   **Default:** 1

Sets the level of Samba log messages to send to syslog. Higher is more verbose. The *syslog.conf* file must have suitable logging enabled.

syslog only = boolean   **[global]**

Allowable values: YES, NO   **Default:** NO

If set to YES, logs only to syslog instead of the standard Samba log files.

template homedir = path   **[global]**

Allowable values: full path to directory   **Default:** /home/%D/%U

Sets the home directory for Unix login sessions for users authenticated through winbind. %D will be replaced with user's domain name; %U by the username.

template shell = filename   **[global]**

Allowable values: full path to shell   **Default:** /bin/false

Sets the shell for Unix login sessions for users authenticated through winbind. The default value prevents all Windows domain user logins.

time offset = number   **[global]**

Allowable values: number of minutes   **Default:** 0

Sets the number of minutes to add to the system time zone calculation. Provided to fix a client daylight-savings bug. Not recommended.

time server = boolean [global]

Allowable values: YES, NO **Default:** NO

If set to YES, *nmbd* advertises itself as a provider of SMB time service to clients. This option only affects whether the time service is advertised. It does not enable or disable time service.

timestamp logs = boolean [global]

Allowable values: YES, NO **Default:** YES

Synonym for debug timestamp.

total print jobs = number [global]

Allowable values: number **Default:** 0 (no limit)

Limits total number of current print jobs on server. See also max print jobs.

unix extensions = boolean [global]

Allowable values: YES, NO **Default:** NO

If set to YES, supports CIFS Unix extensions, providing better file-system support for Unix clients. Obsolete in Samba 3.0, which always offers support.

unix password sync = boolean [global]

Allowable values: YES, NO **Default:** NO

If set to YES, attempts to change the user's Unix password whenever the user changes her SMB password. Used to ease synchronization of Unix and Microsoft password databases. See also password program and passwd chat.

update encrypted = boolean [global]

Allowable values: YES, NO **Default:** NO

Updates the encrypted password file when a user logs on with an unencrypted password. Provided to ease conversion from unencrypted to encrypted passwords.

use client driver = boolean   [global]

Allowable values: YES, NO   **Default:** NO

Used for avoiding Access Denied; Unable to connect messages
when connecting to a Samba printer from Windows NT/2000/XP
clients. Necessary only when the client has a local printer driver
for the Samba printer.

use mmap = boolean   [global]

Allowable values: YES, NO   **Default:** (varies)

Tells Samba whether the *mmap()* system call works correctly on
the Samba host. Default is automatically set correctly. Do not
change.

use rhosts = boolean   [global]

Allowable values: YES, NO   **Default:** NO

If set to YES, users' *~/.rhosts* files will be used to identify systems
from which users can connect without providing a password.
Discouraged. Obsolete in Samba 3.0.

use sendfile = boolean

Allowable values: YES, NO   **Default:** NO

If yes, Samba will perform some data transfers for exclusively
oplocked files using the *sendfile()* system call, which results in
significant performance improvements. This is available if Samba
has been configured with the --with-sendfile-support option.
This is an experimental option and is new in Samba 2.2.5.

user = user list

Allowable values: user list   **Default:** (null)

Synonym for username.

username = user list

Allowable values: user list   **Default:** (null)

Sets a list of users that are tried when logging on with share-level
security in effect. Also called user or users. Discouraged. Use the
NET USE *server**share*%*user* list from the client.

username level = number   [global]

Allowable values: number   **Default:** 0

Specifies the number of uppercase-letter permutations allowed to match Unix usernames. A workaround for Windows' single-case usernames. Use is discouraged.

username map = filename   [global]

Allowable values: name of file   **Default:** (null)

Names a file of Unix-to-Windows name pairs; used to map different spellings of account names and Windows usernames longer than eight characters.

users = user list

Allowable values: user list   **Default:** (null)

Synonym for username.

utmp = boolean   [global]

Allowable values: YES, NO   **Default:** NO

This is available if Samba has been configured with the --with-utmp option. If set, Samba adds *utmp/utmpx* records whenever a connection is made to a Samba server. Sites can use this option to record each connection to a Samba share as a system login.

utmp directory = directory   [global]

Allowable values: name of directory   **Default:** (null)

This is available if Samba has been configured with the --with-utmp option. If this option and utmp are set, Samba will look in the specified directory rather than the default system directory for *utmp/utmpx* files.

valid chars = list

Allowable values: list of numeric values   **Default:** (null)

Adds national characters to a character set map. See also client code page. Obsolete in Samba 3.0.

valid users = user list

Allowable values: user list   **Default:** (null—allows everyone)

Specifies a list of users that can connect to a share. See also invalid users.

veto files = slash-separated list

Allowable values: slash-separated list of filenames   **Default:** (null)

Specifies a list of files that the client will not see when listing a directory's contents. See also delete veto files and hide files.

veto oplock files = slash-separated list

Allowable values: slash-separated list of filenames   **Default:** (null)

Specifies a list of files not to oplock (and cache on clients). See also oplocks and fake oplocks.

vfs object = filename

Allowable values: full path to shared library   **Default:** (null)

Specifies the shared library to use for Samba's Virtual File System (VFS). Requires the --with-vfs configure option.

vfs options = string

Allowable values: space-separated list of options   **Default:** (null)

Specifies parameters to the VFS. Requires the --with-vfs configure option. See vfs object.

volume = string

Allowable values: share name   **Default:** (null)

Sets the volume label of a disk share. Especially useful with shared CD-ROMs.

wide links = boolean

Allowable values: YES, NO   **Default:** YES

If set, Samba follows symlinks out of the disk share. See also the root dir and follow symlinks options.

winbind cache time = number [global]

Allowable values: number of seconds   **Default:** 15

Sets the amount of time that the *winbindd* daemon caches user and group information.

winbind enum groups = boolean [global]

Allowable values: YES, NO   **Default:** YES

If set to NO, enumeration of groups is suppressed by winbind. Discouraged.

winbind enum users = boolean [global]

Allowable values: YES, NO   **Default:** YES

If set to NO, enumeration of users is suppressed by winbind. Discouraged.

winbind gid = numeric range [global]

Allowable values: integer–integer   **Default:** (null)

Specifies the group ID range winbind uses for Windows NT domain users connecting to Samba.

winbind separator = character [global]

Allowable values: ASCII character   **Default:** \

Specifies the character winbind uses to separate a domain name and username.

winbind uid = numeric range [global]

Allowable values: integer-integer   **Default:** (null)

Specifies the user ID range winbind will use for Windows NT domain users connecting to Samba.

wins hook = command [global]

Allowable values: full path to script   **Default:** (null)

Specifies a command to run whenever the WINS server updates its database. Allows WINS to be synchronized with DNS or other services. The command is passed one of the arguments add, delete, or refresh, followed by the NetBIOS name, the name type (two hexadecimal digits), the TTL in seconds, and the IP addresses corresponding to the NetBIOS name. Requires wins service = YES.

wins proxy = boolean   [global]

Allowable values: YES, NO   **Default:** NO

If set to YES, *nmbd* proxies resolution requests to WINS servers on behalf of old clients, which use broadcasts. The WINS server is typically on another subnet.

wins server = value   [global]

Allowable values: hostname or IP address   **Default:** (null)

Sets the DNS name or IP address of the WINS server.

wins support = boolean   [global]

Allowable values: YES, NO   **Default:** NO

If set to YES, activates the WINS service. The wins server option must not be set if wins support = YES.

workgroup = name   [global]

Allowable values: workgroup name   **Default:** WORKGROUP

Sets the workgroup or domain to which the Samba server belongs. Overrides the compiled-in default of WORKGROUP. Choosing a name other than WORKGROUP is highly recommended.

writable = boolean

Allowable values: YES, NO   **Default:** YES

Antonym for read only; writeable and write ok are synonyms.

writeable = boolean

Allowable values: YES, NO   **Default:** YES

Antonym for read only; writable and write ok are synonyms.

write cache size = number

Allowable values: decimal number of bytes   **Default:** 0 (disabled)

Allocates a write buffer of the specified size in which Samba accumulates data before a write to disk. This option can be used to ensure that each write has the optimal size for a given filesystem. It is typically used with RAID drives, which have a preferred write size, and with systems that have large memory and slow disks.

write list = user list

Allowable values: user list   **Default:** (null)

Specifies a list of users that are given read/write access to a read-only share. See also read list.

write ok = boolean

Allowable values: YES, NO   **Default:** YES

Synonym for writable.

write raw = boolean   [global]

Allowable values: YES, NO   **Default:** YES

Allows fast-streaming writes over TCP using 64KB buffers. Recommended.

Glossary of Configuration Value Types

boolean
> One of two values, either YES or NO.

character
> A single ASCII character.

command
> A Unix script or compiled program, with an absolute path specified for the executable and parameters.

directory
>An absolute path specification to a directory. For example:
>```
>/usr/local/samba/lib
>```

filename
>An absolute path specification to a file. For example:
>```
>/etc/printcap
>```

host list
>A list of hosts. Allows IP addresses, address masks, domain names, ALL, and EXCEPT.

interface list
>A list of interfaces, in either address/netmask or address/n-bits format. For example:
>```
>192.168.2.10/255.255.255.0, 192.168.2.10/24
>```

map list
>A list of filename remapping strings. For example:
>```
>(*.html *.htm)
>```

name
>A single name of a type of object, as specified in the option's description.

number
>A positive integer.

numeric range
>Two numbers separated by a dash, specifying a minimum and a maximum value. For example:
>```
>100-250
>```

remote list
>A list of subnet-broadcast-address/workgroup pairs. For example:
>```
>192.168.2.255/SERVERS 192.168.4.255/STAFF
>```

service (share) list
>A list of service (share) names, without the enclosing parentheses.

slash-separated list
> A list of filenames, separated by "/" characters to allow embedded spaces. For example:
>
>   /.*/My Documents/*.doc/

string
> One line of arbitrary text.

user list
> A list of usernames and/or group names. *@group_name* includes whomever is in the NIS netgroup *group_name*, if one exists, or otherwise whomever is in the Unix group *group_name*. In addition, *+group_name* is a Unix group, *&group_name* is an NIS netgroup, and &+ and +& cause an ordered search of both Unix and NIS groups.

value
> A value of some miscellaneous type, as specified in the option's description.

Configuration File Variables

Table 1 lists the Samba configuration file variables.

Table 1. Configuration file variables

Name	Meaning
%a	Client's architecture (Samba, WfWg, WinNT, Win95, or UNKNOWN)
%d	Current server process's process ID
%D	User's Windows NT Domain
%f	Printer spool file as a relative path (printing only)
%f	User from which a message was sent (messages only)
%G	Primary group name of %U (requested username)
%g	Primary group name of %u (actual username)
%H	Home directory of %u (actual username)

Table 1. Configuration file variables (continued)

Name	Meaning
%h	Samba server's (Internet) hostname
%I	Client's IP address
%j	Print job number (printing only)
%L	Samba server's NetBIOS name (virtual servers have multiple names)
%M	Client's (Internet) hostname
%m	Client's NetBIOS name
%N	Name of the NIS home directory server (without NIS, same as %L)
%n	New password (password change only)
%o	Old password (password change only)
%P	Current share's root directory (actual)
%p	Current share's root directory (in an NIS homedir map)
%p	Print filename (printing only)
%R	Protocol level in use (CORE, COREPLUS, LANMAN1, LANMAN2, or NT1)
%S	Current share's name
%s	Name of the file in which the message resides (messages only)
%s	Printer spool filename (printing only)
%T	Current date and time
%t	Destination system (messages only)
%U	Requested username for current share
%u	Current share's username
%v	Samba version
%$(name)	Value of environment variable *name*

Samba Daemons

The following sections provide information about the command-line parameters for *smbd*, *nmbd*, and *winbindd*.

smbd

`smbd [options]`

The *smbd* program provides Samba's file and printer services, using one TCP/IP stream and one daemon per client. It is controlled from */usr/local/samba/lib/smb.conf*, the default configuration file, which can be overridden by command-line options.

The configuration file is automatically reevaluated every minute. If it has changed, most new options are immediately effective. You can force Samba to reload the configuration file immediately by sending a SIGHUP signal to *smbd*. Reloading the configuration file does not affect any clients that are already connected. To escape this condition, a client would need to disconnect and reconnect, or the server itself would have to be restarted, forcing all clients to reconnect.

Other signals

To shut down an *smbd* process, send it the termination signal SIGTERM (15), which allows it to die gracefully, instead of a SIGKILL (9). With Samba versions prior to 2.2, the debugging level could be raised or lowered using SIGUSR1 or SIGUSR2. This is no longer supported. Use *smbcontrol* instead.

Options

`-a`

Causes each new connection to the Samba server to append all logging messages to the log file. This option is the opposite of `-o` and is the default.

`-D`

Runs the *smbd* program as a daemon. This is the recommended way to use *smbd*. It is also the default action when *smbd* is run from an interactive command line. In addition, *smbd* can be run from *inetd*.

`-d debug_level`

Sets the debug (sometimes called logging) level. The level can range from 0 to 10. Specifying the value on the command line overrides the value specified in the *smb.conf* file. Debug level 0 logs only the most important messages; level 1 is normal; levels 3 and above are primarily for debugging and slow *smbd* considerably.

-h

Prints usage information for the *smbd* command.

-i

Runs *smbd* interactively, rather than as a daemon. This option is used to override the default daemon mode when *smbd* is run from the command line.

-l *log_directory*

Sends the log messages to somewhere other than the location compiled into the executable or specified in the *smb.conf* file. The default is often */usr/local/samba/var/*, */usr/samba/var/*, or */var/log/*. The log file is placed in the specified directory and named *log.smbd*. If the directory does not exist, Samba's compiled-in default will be used.

-O *socket_options*

Sets the TCP/IP socket options, using the same parameters as the socket options configuration option. Often used for performance tuning and testing.

-o

Causes log files to be overwritten when opened (the opposite of -a). Using this option saves you from hunting for the right log entries if you are performing a series of tests and inspecting the log file each time.

-p *port_number*

Sets the TCP/IP port number from which the server will accept requests. All Microsoft clients send to the default port of 139 (except for Windows 2000/XP, which can use port 445 for SMB networking without the NetBIOS protocol layer).

-P

Causes *smbd* to run in "passive" mode, in which it just listens, and does not transmit any network traffic. This is useful only for debugging by developers.

-s *configuration_file*

Specifies the location of the Samba configuration file. Although the file defaults to */usr/local/samba/lib/smb.conf*, you can override it on the command line. Typically used for debugging.

-v

Prints the current version of Samba.

nmbd

nmbd *[options]*

The *nmbd* program is Samba's NetBIOS name service and browsing daemon. It replies to NetBIOS over TCP/IP (also called NetBT or NBT) name-service requests broadcast from SMB clients, and optionally to Microsoft's Windows Internet Name Service (WINS) requests. Both are versions of the name-to-address lookup required by SMB clients. The broadcast version uses UDP broadcast on the local subnet only, while WINS uses TCP, which can be routed. If running as a WINS server, *nmbd* keeps a current name and address database in the file */usr/local/samba/var/locks/wins.dat*.

An active *nmbd* daemon also responds to browsing protocol requests used by the Windows Network Neighborhood. This protocol provides a dynamic directory of servers, as well as the disks and printers that the servers are providing. As with WINS, this was initially done by making UDP broadcasts on the local subnet. With the addition of the local master browser to the network architecture, it is done by making TCP connections to a server. If *nmbd* is acting as a local master browser, it stores the browsing database in the file */usr/local/samba/var/locks/browse.dat*.

Some clients (especially older ones) cannot use the WINS protocol. To support these clients, *nmbd* can act as a WINS proxy, accepting broadcast requests from the non-WINS clients, contacting a WINS server on their behalf, and returning the WINS server's response to them.

Signals

Like *smbd*, the *nmbd* program responds to several Unix signals. Sending *nmbd* a SIGHUP signal causes it to dump the names it knows about to the */usr/local/samba/var/locks/namelist.debug* file. To shut down an *nmbd* process and allow it to die gracefully, send it a SIGTERM (15) signal, rather than a SIGKILL (9). With Samba versions prior to 2.2, the debugging level could be raised or lowered using SIGUSR1 or SIGUSR2. This is no longer supported. Use *smbcontrol* instead.

Options

-a

Causes each new connection to the Samba server to append all logging messages to the log file. This option is the opposite of -o and is the default.

-d *debug_level*

Sets the debug (sometimes called logging) level. The level can range from 0 to 10. Specifying the value on the command line overrides the value specified in the *smb.conf* file. Debug level 0 logs only the most important messages; level 1 is normal; levels 3 and above are primarily for debugging and slow *nmbd* considerably.

-D

Instructs the *nmbd* program to run as a daemon. This is the recommended way to use *nmbd* and is the default when *nmbd* is run from an interactive shell. In addition, *nmbd* can be run from *inetd*.

-h

Prints usage information for the *nmbd* command.

-H *lmhosts_file*

Specifies the location of the *lmhosts* file for name resolution. This file is used only to resolve names for the local server, and not to answer queries from remote systems. The compiled-in default is commonly */usr/local/samba/lib/lmhosts*, */usr/samba/lib/lmhosts*, or */etc/lmhosts*.

-i

Runs *nmbd* interactively, rather than as a daemon. This option is used to override the default daemon mode when *nmbd* is run from the command line.

-l *log_file*

Sends the log messages to somewhere other than the location compiled into the executable or specified in the *smb.conf* file. The default is often */usr/local/samba/var/log.nmbd*, */usr/samba/var/log.nmbd*, or */var/log/log.nmbd*.

-n *NetBIOS_name*

Allows you to override the NetBIOS name by which the daemon advertises itself. Specifying this option on the command line overrides the netbios name option in the Samba configuration file.

-O *socket_options*

> Sets the TCP/IP socket options, using the same parameters as the socket options configuration option. Often used for performance tuning and testing.

-o

> Causes log files to be overwritten when opened (the opposite of -a). This option saves you from hunting for the right log entries if you are performing a series of tests and inspecting the log file each time.

-p *port_number*

> Sets the UDP port number from which the server accepts requests. Currently, all Microsoft clients use only the default port, 137.

-s *configuration_file*

> Specifies the location of the Samba configuration file. Although the file defaults to */usr/local/samba/lib/smb.conf*, you can override it here on the command line. Typically used for debugging.

-v

> Prints the current version of Samba.

winbindd

winbindd *[options]*

The *winbindd* daemon is part of the winbind service and is used to allow Unix systems to obtain user and group information from a Windows NT/2000 server. Winbind maps Windows relative IDs (RIDs) to Unix UIDs and GIDs and allows accounts stored on the Windows server to be used for Unix authentication. Its purpose is to ease integration of Microsoft and Unix networks when a preexisting Windows domain controller is set up to handle user and computer accounts.

The daemon is accessed by users via the name service switch and PAM. The name service switch calls a library (*/lib/libnss_winbind. so*), which calls the daemon, which in turn calls the Windows NT/ 2000 server using Microsoft RPC. The PAM module for winbind can call the daemon similarly, allowing users whose accounts are stored on the Windows server to log in to the Unix system and run an interactive shell, FTP, or any other program that authenticates users through PAM.

The winbind subsystem is currently available only for the Linux operating system and a few other systems that use shared libraries, nsswitch and PAM.

Options

-d *debuglevel*

> Sets the debug (sometimes called logging) level. The level can range from 0 to 10. Specifying the value on the command line overrides the value specified in the *smb.conf* file. Debug level 0 logs only the most important messages; level 1 is normal; levels 3 and above are primarily for debugging.

-i

> Runs *winbindd* interactively. This option is used to override the default, which is for winbindd to detach and run as a daemon.

Samba Distribution Programs

This section lists the command-line options and subcommands provided by each nondaemon program in the Samba distribution.

findsmb

findsmb [*subnet_broadcast_address*]

This Perl script reports information about systems on the subnet that respond to SMB name-query requests. The report includes the IP address, NetBIOS name, workgroup/domain, and operating system of each system.

If a different subnet's broadcast address is provided, it will find SMB servers on that subnet. If no subnet broadcast address is supplied, *findsmb* will look on the local subnet.

The system with an asterisk (*) in front of its workgroup name is the domain master browser for the workgroup/domain, and the system with a plus sign (+) preceding its workgroup name is the local master browser.

The *findsmb* command was introduced during the development of Samba 2.2 and is installed by default in Samba Versions 2.2.5 and later.

make_smbcodepage

```
make_smbcodepage c/d codepage_number input_file output_file
```

This program is part of the internationalization features of Samba 2.2 and is obsolete in Samba 3.0, which supports Unicode automatically. The *make_smbcodepage* program compiles a binary codepage file from a text-format codepage definition. It can also perform the reverse operation, decompiling a binary codepage file into a text version. Examples of text-format codepage files can be found in the Samba distribution in the *source/codepages* directory. After Samba has been installed, examples of binary codepages can be found in the directory */usr/local/samba/lib/codepages*.

For the first argument, use c to compile a codepage and d to decompile a codepage file. The `codepage_number` argument is the number of the codepage being processed (e.g., 850). The `input_file` and `output_file` are the text- and binary-format codepages, with the types dependent on the operation (compiling or decompiling) that is being performed.

make_unicodemap

```
make_unicodemap codepage_number inputfile outputfile
```

This program is part of the internationalization features of Samba 2.2 and is obsolete in Samba 3.0, which supports Unicode automatically. The *make_unicodemap* command compiles binary Unicode maps from text files, so Samba can display non-ASCII characters in file and directory names via the Unicode international alphabets. Examples of input mapping files can be found in the directory *source/codepages* in the Samba source distribution.

The input file is an ASCII map; the output file is a binary file loadable by Samba. The codepage is the number of the DOS codepage (e.g., 850) for the map.

net

net *[method]* *function* *[misc_options]* *[target_options]*

The *net* command, new to Samba 3.0, is a program with a syntax similar to the MS-DOS/Windows command of the same name. It is used for performing various administrative functions related to Windows networking, which can be executed either locally or on a remote system.

The *function* argument is made up of one or more space-separated words. In Windows terminology, it is sometimes referred to as a function with options. Here we list every function in its complete form, including multiple words.

By default, the action is performed on the local system. The *target_options* argument can be used to specify a remote system (either by hostname or IP address), a domain, or a workgroup.

Depending on the function, the *method* argument can be optional, required, or disallowed. It specifies one of three methods for performing the operation specified by the rest of the command. It can be ads (Active Directory), rpc (Microsoft's DCE/RPC), or rap (Microsoft's original SMB remote procedure call). To determine which methods (if any) can be used with a function, the net help ads, net help rap, and net help rpc commands can be used to list the functions for each method.

Miscellaneous options

-d *level*
--debug=*level*
> Sets the debug (sometimes called logging) level. The level can range from 0 to 10.

-l
--long
> Specifies the long listing mode. This is provided for functions that print informational listings.

-n *name*
--myname=*name*
> Specifies the NetBIOS name for the client.

-p *port*
--port=*port*
> Specifies the port number to use.

-s *filename*
--conf=*filename*
> Specifies the name of the Samba configuration file, overriding the compiled-in default.

-U *username[%password]*
--user=*username[%password]*
> Specifies the username and, optionally, the password to use for functions that require authentication.

-W *name*
--myworkgroup=*name*
> Specifies the name of the client's workgroup, overriding the definition of the workgroup parameter in the Samba configuration file.

Target options

-S *hostname*
> Specifies the remote system using a hostname or NetBIOS name.

-I *ip_address*
> Specifies the remote system using its IP address.

-w *workgroup*
> Specifies the name of the target domain or workgroup.

Functions

abortshutdown
> See the rpc abortshutdown function.

ads info
> Prints information about the Active Directory server. The method (ads) must be specified to differentiate this function from the rpc info function.

ads join *OU*
> Joins the local system to the Active Directory realm (organizational unit) specified by OU. The method (ads) must be specified to differentiate this function from the rpc join function.

ads leave
> Removes the local system from the Active Directory realm.

`ads` password *username@REALM* -U*admin_username@REALM%admin_password*

> Changes the Active Directory password for the user specified by *username@REALM*. The administrative account authentication information is specified with the -U option. The Active Directory realm must be supplied in all uppercase.

`ads` printer info *[printer] [server]*

> Prints information on the specified printer on the specified server. The *printer* argument defaults to an asterisk (*), meaning all printers, and the *server* argument defaults to localhost.

`ads` printer publish *printer_name*

> Publishes the specified printer in Active Directory.

`ads` printer remove *printer_name*

> Removes the specified printer from Active Directory.

`ads` search *expr attrib*

> Performs a raw Active Directory search, using the standard LDAP search expression and attributes specified by the *expr* and *attrib* arguments, respectively.

`ads` status

> Prints details about the Active Directory computer account of the system.

change localhost pass

> Changes the Active Directory password for the local system's computer trust account.

domain

> Lists the domains or workgroups on the network.

file

> Lists open files on the server.

file close *file_id*

> Closes the specified file.

file info *file_id*

> Prints information about the specified file, which must be open.

file user *username*

> Lists all files opened on the server by the user specified by *username*.

`group add` *group_name*
> Adds the specified group. This function accepts the miscellaneous option -C *comment* (which can also be specified as --comment=*string*) to set the descriptive comment for the group.

`group delete` *group_name*
> Deletes the specified group.

`groupmember add` *group_name username*
> Adds the user specified by *username* to the group specified by *group_name*.

`groupmember delete` *group_name username*
> Deletes the user specified by *username* from the group specified by *group_name*.

`groupmember list` *group_name*
> Lists the users who are members of the specified group.

`help`
> Prints a help message for the *net* command.

`help` *method*
> Prints a help message for *method*, which can be ads, rap, or rpc. This lists the functions that can use the method, along with a brief description.

`help` *function*
> Prints a help message for the specified function, which can be more than one word.

`info`
> Must be preceded by a method. See the ads info and rpc info functions.

`join`
> Joins the computer to a Windows NT domain or Active Directory realm. If the method argument is not specified, a check is made to determine if Active Directory is in use, and if so, ads join is performed. Otherwise, rpc join is run. See also the ads join and rpc join functions.

`leave`
> Must be preceded by a method. See the ads leave function.

`lookup dc [domain]`
> Prints the IP address of the specified domain's domain controllers. The domain defaults to the value of the `workgroup` parameter in the Samba configuration file.

`lookup host hostname [type]`
> Prints the IP address of the specified host.

`lookup kdc [realm]`
> Prints the IP address of the specified realm's Kerberos domain controller. If `realm` is not specified, it defaults to the value of the `realm` parameter in the Samba configuration file.

`lookup ldap [domain]`
> Prints the IP address of the specified domain's LDAP server. If `domain` is not specified, it defaults to the value of the `workgroup` parameter in the Samba configuration file.

`lookup master [domain]`
> Prints the IP address of the master browser of the specified domain or workgroup. If `domain` is not specified, it defaults to the value of the `workgroup` parameter in the Samba configuration file.

`password username old_password new_password`
> Changes the password for the user specified by the `username` argument. The user's old and new passwords are provided in plain text as part of the command. Be careful regarding security issues. See also the `ads password` function.

`printer info`
> See the `ads printer info` function.

`printer publish`
> See the `ads printer publish` function.

`printer remove`
> See the `ads printer remove` function.

`printq`
> Prints information (including the job IDs) about printer queues on the server.

`printq delete queue_name`
> Deletes the specified printer queue. The `-j job_id` (which can also be specified as `--jobid=job_id`) option may be used to specify the job ID of the queue.

rpc abortshutdown
:   Aborts the shutdown of a remote server.

rpc info
:   Prints information about the server's domain. The method (rpc) must be specified to differentiate this function from the ads info function.

rpc join
:   Joins a computer to a Windows NT domain. If the -U *username%password* option is included, the specified username and password will be used as the administrative account required for authenticating with the PDC. If the -U option is not included, this function can be used only to join the computer to the domain after the computer account has been created using the Server Manager. The method (rpc) must be specified to differentiate this function from the ads join function.

rpc shutdown
:   Shuts down a server. This function accepts the -r, -f, -t, and -c miscellaneous options. The -r option (which can also be specified as --reboot) requests that the system reboot after shutting down. The -f option (which can also be specified as --force) forces a shutdown. The -t *timeout* option (which can also be specified as --timeout=*number*) specifies the number of seconds to wait before shutting down, and the -c *comment* option (which can also be specified as --comment=*string*) can be used to specify a message to the client user. On Windows, the comment appears in the Message area in the System Shutdown dialog box.

rpc trustdom add *domain_name*
:   Adds an account for the trust relationship with the specified Windows NT domain.

rpc trustdom establish *domain_name*
:   Establishes a trust relationship with the specified Windows NT domain.

rpc trustdom revoke *domain_name*
:   Revokes the trust relationship with the specified Windows NT domain.

search
:   See the ads search function.

---

server

Lists servers in the domain or workgroup, which defaults to the value of the `workgroup` parameter in the Samba configuration file.

session

Lists clients with open sessions to the server.

session delete *NetBIOS_name*

Closes the session to the server from the specified client. A synonym is `session close`.

session close

A synonym for `session delete`.

share

Lists the shares offered by the server. When a Windows 95/98/Me server is the target system, it might be necessary to specify the method as `rap` for this to work properly.

share add *share_name=server_path*

Adds a share on the target server. The name of the share and the folder to be shared are specified by the *share_name=server_path* argument, with *server_path* the Windows directory name, with spaces and other special characters (if any) quoted and with the backslashes escaped (e.g., `"data=C:\\Documents and Settings\\jay\\Desktop\\data"`). The `-C` *comment* option (which can also be specified as `--comment=`*string*) can be used to define a description for the share. The `-M` *number* option (which can also be specified as `--maxusers=`*number*) can be used to set the maximum number of users that can connect to the share. The method (`rap` or `rpc`) might need to be specified for this function to work. The regular folder icon cannot change into a "shared folder" icon in Windows Explorer until the display is refreshed.

share delete *share_name*

Deletes a share from the target server. The *share_name* argument is simply the name of the share on the target server, not a UNC. The method (`rap` or `rpc`) might need to be specified for this function to work. The "shared folder" icon in Windows Explorer cannot change back to the regular folder icon until the display is refreshed.

shutdown

See the `rpc shutdown` function.

status
> See the ads status function.

time
> Displays the system time (in Unix *date* command format) on the target system.

time set
> Sets the local system's hardware clock using the time obtained from the operating system.

time system
> Sets the time on the local system using the time obtained from the remote system.

time zone
> Prints the time zone (in hours from GMT) in use on the system.

trustdom add
> See the rpc trustdom add function.

trustdom establish
> See the rpc trustdom establish function.

trustdom revoke
> See the rpc trustdom revoke function.

user
> Lists user accounts. The method can be specified as ads, rap, or rpc.

user add *username [password]*
> Adds a user account for the user specified by *username*. The -c *comment* option (also specified as --comment=*string*) can be used to set a comment for the account. The -F *user_flags* option can be used to set flags (specified in numeric format) for the account. The method can be specified as ads, rap, or rpc.

user delete *username*
> Deletes the specified user's account. The method can be specified as ads, rap, or rpc.

user info *username*
> Lists the domain groups to which the specified user belongs. The method can be specified as ads, rap, or rpc.

nmblookup

nmblookup [options] netbios_name

The *nmblookup* program is a client program that allows command-line access to NetBIOS name service for resolving NetBIOS computer names into IP addresses. The program works by broadcasting its queries on the local subnet until a machine with the specified name responds. You can think of it as a Windows analog of *nslookup* or *dig*. This is useful for looking up regular computer names, as well as special-purpose names, such as __MSBROWSE__. If you wish to query for a particular type of NetBIOS name, add the NetBIOS type to the end of the name, using the format *netbios_name#<dd>*.

Options

-A

Interprets *netbios_name* as an IP address and does a node status query on it.

-B *broadcast_address*

Sends the query to the given broadcast address. The default is to send the query to the broadcast address of the primary network interface.

-d *debug_level*

Sets the debug (sometimes called logging) level. The level can range from 0 to 10. Debug level 0 logs only the most important messages. Level 1 is normal; levels 3 and above are primarily used by developers for debugging the *nmblookup* program itself and slow the program considerably.

-f

Prints the flags in the packet headers.

-h

Prints command-line usage information for the program.

-i *scope*

Sets a NetBIOS scope identifier. NetBIOS scope is a rarely used precursor to workgroups.

-M

Searches for a local master browser by looking up *netbios_name<1d>*. If *netbios_name* is specified as a dash (-), a lookup is done on the special name __MSBROWSE__.

-R

Sets the "recursion desired" bit in the packet. This causes the system that responds to try a WINS lookup and return the address and any other information the WINS server has saved.

-r

Uses the root port of 137. This option exists as a bug workaround for Windows 95. This option might require the user to be superuser.

-S

Performs a node status query once the name query has returned an IP address. This returns all the resource types that the system knows about, including their numeric attributes. For example:

```
$ nmblookup -S toltec
querying toltec on 172.16.1.255
172.16.1.1 toltec<00>
Looking up status of 172.16.1.1
        TOLTEC          <00> -          M <ACTIVE>
        TOLTEC          <03> -          M <ACTIVE>
        TOLTEC          <20> -          M <ACTIVE>
        ..__MSBROWSE__. <01> - <GROUP> M <ACTIVE>
        METRAN          <00> - <GROUP> M <ACTIVE>
        METRAN          <1b> -          M <ACTIVE>
        METRAN          <1c> - <GROUP> M <ACTIVE>
        METRAN          <1d> -          M <ACTIVE>
        METRAN          <1e> - <GROUP> M <ACTIVE>
```

-s *configuration_file*

Specifies the location of the Samba configuration file. Although the file defaults to */usr/local/samba/lib/smb.conf*, you can override it here on the command line. Normally used for debugging.

-T

Translates IP addresses into resolved names.

-U *unicast_address*

Performs a unicast query to the specified address. Used with -R to query WINS servers.

Note that *nmblookup* has no option for setting the workgroup. You can get around this by putting workgroup = *workgroup_name* in a file and passing it to *nmblookup* with the -s option.

pdbedit

pdbedit [options]

This program, new to Samba 3.0, can be used to manage accounts that are held in a SAM database. The implementation of the database can be any of the types supported by Samba, including the *smbpasswd* file, LDAP, NIS+ and the *tdb* database library. The user must be the superuser to use this tool.

Options

-a

Adds the user specified by the -u option to the SAM database. The command issues a prompt for the user's password.

-d *drive_letter*

Sets the Windows drive letter to which to map the user's home directory. The drive letter should be specified as a letter followed by a colon—e.g., H:.

-D *debug_level*

Sets the debug (sometimes called logging) level. The level can range from 0 to 10. Debug level 0 logs only the most important messages. Level 1 is normal, and levels 3 and above are primarily for debugging.

-e *pwdb_backend*

Exports the user account database to another format, written to the specified location. Used for migrating from one type of account database to another. The *pwdb_backend* argument is specified in the format of a database type, followed by a colon, then the location of the database. For example, to export the existing account database to an *smbpasswd* database in the file */usr/local/samba/private/smbpw*, *pwdb_backend* would be specified as smbpasswd:/usr/local/samba/private/smbpw. The allowable database types are smbpasswd, smbpasswd nua, tdbsam, tdbsam nua, ldapsam, ldapsam_nua, and plugin.

-f *full_name*

Sets the full name of the user specified with the -u option.

-h *unc*

Sets the home directory path (as a UNC) for the user specified with the -u option.

-i *pwdb_backend*

Specifies a password database backend from which to retrieve account information, overriding the one specified by the passdb backend parameter in the Samba configuration file. This, along with the -e option, is useful for migrating user accounts from one type of account database to another. See the -e option regarding how to specify the *pwdb_backend* argument.

-l

Lists the user accounts in the database. See also the -v option.

-m

Indicates that the account is a computer account rather than a user account. Used only with the -a option when creating the account. In this case, the -u option specifies the computer name rather than a username.

-p *unc*

Sets the directory in which the user's profile is kept. The directory is specified as a UNC.

-s *unc*

Specifies the UNC of the user's logon script.

-u *username*

Specifies the username of the account to add (with the -a option), delete (with the -x option), or modify.

-v

Selects verbose mode when listing accounts with the -l option. The account fields will be printed.

-w

Selects the smbpasswd listing mode, for use with the -l option, which prints information in the same format as it would appear in an *smbpasswd* file.

-x

Deletes the user (specified with the -u option) from the account database.

rpcclient

rpcclient *server [options]*

This is a program for issuing administrative commands that are implemented using Microsoft RPCs. It provides access to the

RPCs that Windows administrative GUIs use for system management. The *rpcclient* command is mainly for use by advanced users who understand the RPCs. More information on these can be found in Microsoft's Platform Software Development Kit (SDK), available for download from the Microsoft web site at *http://www.microsoft.com*.

You can run a single *rpcclient* command by using the -c command string option, or interactively with *rpcclient* prompting for commands.

Options

-A *filename*

Specifies a file from which to read the authentication values used in the connection. The format of the file is as follows:

```
username = value
password = value
domain   = value
```

This option is used to avoid password prompts or to have the password appear in plain text inside scripts. The permissions on the file should be very restrictive (0600, for example) to prevent access from unwanted users.

-c *command_string*

Executes a sequence of semicolon-separated commands. Commands are listed in the following section.

-d *debuglevel*

Sets the debug (sometimes called logging) level. The level can range from 0 to 10. Specifying the value on the command line overrides the value specified in the *smb.conf* file. Debug level 0 logs only the most important messages; level 1 is normal; levels 3 and above are primarily for debugging and slow the program considerably.

-h

Prints a summary of options.

-l *logbasename*

Sets the filename for log/debug files. The extension *.client* is appended to the filename.

-N
   Does not prompt for a password. This is used when Samba is
   configured for share-mode security and a service with no
   password is being accessed.

-s *filename*
   Specifies the location of the Samba configuration file, which
   by default is usually */usr/local/samba/lib/smb.conf*.

-U *username[%password]*
   Sets the SMB username or username and password to use. Be
   careful when specifying the password with *%password*; this is a
   major security risk. If *%password* is not specified, the user will
   be prompted for the password, which will not be echoed.
   Normally the user is set from the USER or LOGNAME environment variable. The -U option by itself means to use the
   guest account. See also -A.

-W *domain*
   Sets the domain, overriding the workgroup parameter in the
   Samba configuration file. If the domain is the server's
   NetBIOS name, it causes the client to log on using the server's
   local SAM database rather than the SAM of the domain.

rpcclient commands

Aside from a few miscellaneous commands, the *rpcclient*
commands fall into three groups: LSARPC, SAMR, and
SPOOLSS. The function names mentioned in some of the
commands are those documented in the Microsoft Platform SDK.

General commands

debuglevel *level*
   Sets the debugging level to *level*. With no argument, the
   current debugging level is printed.

help
   Prints help on the commands.

quit
   Exits *rpcclient*. A synonym is exit.

Local Security Authority Remote Procedure Calls (LSARPC) commands

enumprivs
> Lists the types of privileges known to this domain.

enumtrust
> Lists the domains trusted by this domain.

getdispname *priv_name*
> Prints information on the privilege named *priv_name*.

lookupsids *name*
> Finds a name that corresponds to a security identifier (SID).

lookupnames *sid*
> Finds the SID for one or more names.

lsaquery
> Queries the LSA object.

lsaenumsid
> Lists SIDs for the local LSA.

lsaquerysecobj
> Prints information on security objects for the LSA.

Security Access Manager RPC (SAMR) commands

createdomuser *username*
> Adds a new user in the domain.

deletedomuser *username*
> Removes a user from the domain.

enumalsgroups *type*
> Lists alias groups in the domain, along with their group RIDs. The *type* argument can be either builtin, to list Windows built-in groups such as Administrators and Power Users, or domain, to list groups in the domain. See also the *queryuseraliases* command.

enumdomgroups
> Lists the groups in the domain, along with their group RIDs.

queryaliasmem *user_rid*
> Prints information regarding alias membership. See also the *queryuseraliases* command.

querydispinfo
> Prints out the account database. The information printed includes the RID, username, and full name of each user. The

RID is printed in hexadecimal notation and can be used in this form for commands that take a RID as an argument.

querydominfo

Prints information regarding the domain. This includes the name of the domain, as well as the number of users, groups, and aliases.

querygroup *group_rid*

Given a group RID, prints the group name, description, number of members, and group description.

queryuser *user_rid*

Given a user RID, prints the corresponding username, full name, and other information pertaining to the user.

queryuseraliases *type user_rid*

Prints aliases for the user. The *type* argument can be either builtin or domain. Aliases are used with the Windows messaging service and act like usernames, but they can be attached to a computer rather than a user. This allows messages intended for a user to be sent to a computer on which the user is either not logged on, or logged on under another username.

queryusergroups *user_rid*

Prints information on each group inhabited by the user.

querygroupmem *group_rid*

Prints the RID and attributes for each member of the group.

samlookupnames *type username*

Looks up the *username* in the SAM database and prints its associated RID. The *type* argument can be either builtin, to look up built-in Windows usernames, or domain, to look up names in the domain.

samlookuprids *type rid*

Looks up *rid* in the SAM database and prints its associated group or username. The *type* argument can be either builtin, to look up built-in Windows usernames, or domain, to look up names in the domain. The RID argument can be given in either 0x*DDD* hexadecimal notation or decimal.

samquerysecobj

Prints information on security objects (such as ACLs) in the SAM database.

Windows NT/2000/XP Printing Services (SPOOLSS) commands

adddriver *arch config_file*

Adds a printer driver to the server. The driver files must already exist in the directory returned by *getdriverdir*. The *arch* argument can be one of Windows 4.0 for Windows 95/98/Me, or Windows NT x86, Windows NT PowerPC, Windows Alpha_AXP, and Windows NT R4000. Others might be introduced in the future.

The *config_file* should contain:

```
Long Printer Name:\
Driver File Name:\
Data File Name:\
Config File Name:\
Help File Name:\
NULL:\
Default Data Type:\
```

followed by a comma-separated list of files. Any empty fields should contain the string NULL.

addprinter *printername sharename drivername port*

Adds a printer on the remote server as *sharename*. The printer driver must already be installed on the server with *adddriver*, and the port must be a valid port name returned by *enumports*.

deldriver *drivername*

Deletes a printer driver (for all architectures) from the server's list of printer drivers.

enumports *[level]*

Prints information regarding the printer ports on the server. The *level* argument can be 1 or 2. Level 1 is the default and prints out only the Port Name. Information level 2 is the Port Name, Monitor Name, Description, and Port Type.

enumdrivers *[level]*

Lists all the printer drivers on the system. The *level* argument specifies the information level. Level 1 is the default and prints the Driver Name(s). Level 2 prints the Version, Driver Name, Architecture, Driver Path, Data File, and Config File. Level 3 prints the contents of Level 2, plus the Help File, one or more Dependent Files, Monitor Name, and Default Data Type.

enumprinters *[level]*

Lists all installed printers, regardless of whether they are shared. The *level* argument specifies the information level. Level 1 is the default, and prints Flags, Name, Description, and Comment. Level 2 prints the Server Name, Printer Name, Share Name, Port Name, Driver Name, Comment, Location, Separator File, Print Processor, Data Type, Parameters, Attributes, Priority, Default Priority, Start Time, Until Time, Status, Current Jobs, Average PPM (pages per minute), and a Security Descriptor.

getdriver *[level] printername*

Prints the printer driver information for the given printer. The *level* argument specifies the information level.

Level 1 is the default, and prints the Driver Name. Level 2 prints the Version, Driver Name, Architecture, Driver Path, Data File, and Config File. Level 3 prints the contents of level 2, plus the Help File, one or more Dependent Files, Monitor Name, and Default Data Type.

getdriverdir *arch*

Retrieves the share name and directory for storing printer driver files for a given architecture. Possible values for *arch* are "Windows 4.0" for Windows 95/98/Me, "Windows NT x86" for Windows NT on Intel, "Windows NT PowerPC" for Windows NT on PowerPC, "Windows Alpha AXP" for Windows NT on Alpha, and "Windows NT R4000" for Windows NT on MIPS. Include the quote marks in the command.

getprinter *printername*

Prints the current printer information. The *level* argument specifies the information level.

openprinter *printername*

Attempts to open and close a specified printer and reports whether it was successful.

setdriver *printername drivername*

Unconditionally updates the printer driver used by an installed printer. Both the printer and printer driver must already be correctly installed on the print server.

setprinter *printername comment*

Assigns a comment string to a printer.

smbcacls

`smbcacls //server/share filename [options]`

This program provides a way of modifying Windows NT ACLs on files and directories shared by the Samba server.

Options

`-A acls`

Adds one or more ACLs to the file or directory. Any ACLs already existing for the file or directory are unchanged.

`-M acls`

Modifies the *mask* of the ACLs specified. Refer to the following section, "Specifying ACLs," for details.

`-D acls`

Deletes the specified ACLs.

`-S acls`

Sets the specified ACLs, deleting any ACLs previously set on the file or directory. The ACLs must contain at least a revision, type, owner, and group.

`-U username`

Sets the username used to connect to the specified service. The user is prompted for a password unless the argument is specified as *username%password*. (Specifying the password on the command line is a security risk.) If `-U domain\\username` is specified, the specified domain or workgroup will be used in place of the one specified in the *smb.conf* file.

`-C username`

Changes the owner of the file or directory. This is a shortcut for `-M OWNER:username`. The *username* argument can be given as a username or a SID in the form S-1-*N-N-D-D-D-R*.

`-G groupname`

Changes the group of the file or directory. This is a shortcut for `-M GROUP:groupname`. The *groupname* argument can be given as a group name or a SID in the form S-1-*N-N-D-D-D-R*.

`-n`

Causes all ACL information to be displayed in numeric format rather than in readable strings.

`-h`

Prints a help message.

Specifying ACLs

In the previous options, the same format is always used when specifying ACLs. An ACL is made up of one or more Access Control Entries (ACEs), separated by either commas or escaped newlines. An ACE can be one of the following:

```
REVISION:revision_number
OWNER:username_or_SID
GROUP:group_name_or_SID
ACL:name_or_SID:type/flags/mask
```

The revision_number should always be 1. The OWNER and GROUP entries can be used to set the owner and group for the file or directory. The names can be the textual ones or SIDs in the form S-1-N-N-D-D-D-R.

The ACL entry specifies what access rights to apply to the file or directory. The name_or_SID field specifies to which user or group the permissions apply and can be supplied either as a textual name or a SID. An ACE can be used to either allow or deny access. The type field is set to 1 to specify a permission to be allowed or 0 for specifying a permission to deny. The mask field is the name of the permission and is one of the following:

R   Read access

W   Write access

X   Execute permission

D   Permission to delete

P   Change permissions on the object

O   Take ownership

The following combined permissions can also be specified:

READ
> Equivalent to RX permissions

CHANGE
> Equivalent to RWXD permissions

FULL
> Equivalent to RWXDPO permissions

The flags field is for specifying how objects in directories are to inherit their default permissions from their parent directory. For files, flags is normally set to 0. For directories, flags is usually set to either 9 or 2.

---

smbclient

```
smbclient //server/share [password] [options]
```

The *smbclient* program is the "Swiss army knife" of the Samba suite. Initially developed as a testing tool, it has become a command shell capable of acting as a general-purpose Unix client, with a command set very similar to that of *ftp*. It offers the following set of functions:

- Interactive file transfer, similar to *ftp*
- Interactive printing to shared SMB printers
- Interactive tar format archiving
- Sending messages on the SMB network
- Batch mode tar format archiving
- "What services do you have?" querying
- Debugging

It is possible to run *smbclient* noninteractively, for use in scripts, by specifying the -c option along with a list of commands to execute. Otherwise, *smbclient* runs in interactive mode, prompting for commands such as this:

```
smb:\>
```

The backslash in the prompt is replaced by the current directory within the share as you change your working directory with *smbclient*'s *cd* command.

Options

-A *authfile*

Specifies a file from which to read the username and password used for the connection. The format of the file is as follows:

```
username = value
password = value
domain   = value
```

This is to avoid having the password prompted for or have it appear in plain text in scripts. The permissions on the file should be very restrictive (0600, for example) to prevent access by unwanted users.

-b *buffer_size*
Sets the size of the buffer used when transferring files. It defaults to 65520 bytes and can be changed as a tuning measure. Generally it should be quite large or set to match the size of the buffer on the remote system. It can be set smaller to work around Windows bugs: some Windows 98 systems work best with a buffer size of 1200.

-B *IP_addr*
Sets the broadcast address.

-c *command_string*
Passes a command string to the *smbclient* command interpreter. The argument consists of a semicolon-separated list of commands to be executed.

-d *debug_level*
Sets the debug (logging) level, from 0 to 10, with A for all. Overrides the value in *smb.conf*. Debug level 0 logs only the most important messages; level 1 is normal; debug levels 3 and above are for debugging and slow *smbclient* considerably.

-D *init_dir*
Upon starting up, causes *smbclient* to change its working directory to *init_dir* on the remote host.

-E
Sends output from commands to *stderr* instead of *stdout*.

-h
Prints the command-line help information (usage) for *smbclient*.

-I *IP_address*
Sets the IP address of the server to which the client connects.

-i *scope*
Sets a NetBIOS scope identifier.

-l *log_file*
Sends the log messages to *log_file* rather than to the log file specified in the Samba configuration file or the compiled-in default.

-L *server*
Lists services (shares) offered by the server. This can be used as a quick way to test an SMB server to see if it is working. If there is a name-service problem, use the -I option to specify the server.

-M *NetBIOS_name*

Allows you to send messages using the Windows messaging protocol. Once a connection is established, you can type your message, pressing Ctrl-D to end. The -U and -I options can be used to control the "From" and "To" parts of the message.

-N

Suppresses the password prompt. Useful when using share mode security and accessing a service that has no password.

-n *NetBIOS_name*

Allows you to override the NetBIOS name by which *smbclient* will advertise itself.

-O *socket_options*

Sets the TCP/IP socket options using the same parameters as the socket options configuration option. Often used for performance tuning and testing.

-p *port_number*

Sets the port number with which *smbclient* will connect.

-R *resolve_order*

Sets the resolve order of the name servers. This option is similar to the resolve order configuration option and can take any of the four parameters lmhosts, host, wins, and bcast, in any order. If more than one is specified, the argument is specified as a space-separated list. This option can be used to test name service by specifying only the name service to be tested.

-s *filename*

Specifies the location of the Samba configuration file. Used for debugging.

-t *terminal_code*

Sets the terminal code for Asian languages.

-T *command_string tarfile*

Runs the tar archiver, which is *gtar* compatible. The tar file that is written to or read from is specified by *tarfile*. The two main commands are c (create) and x (extract), which can be followed by any of these:

a

Resets the archive attribute on files after they have been saved. See also the g option.

b *size*
> Sets the block size for writing the tar file, in 512-byte units.

g
> Backs up only files that have their archive bit set. See also the a option.

I *filename*
> Includes files and directories. This is the default, so specifying this is redundant. To perform pattern matching, see also the r option.

N *filename*
> Backs up only those files newer than *file*.

q
> Suppresses diagnostics.

r
> Performs regular expression matching, which can be used along with the I or E option to include or exclude files.

X *filename*
> Excludes files and directories.

-U *username*
> Sets the username and, optionally, the password used for authentication when connecting to the share.

-W *workgroup*
> Specifies the workgroup/domain in which *smbclient* will claim to be a member.

smbclient commands

help [*smbclient_command*]
> With no command specified, prints a list of available commands. If a command is specified as an argument, a brief help message will be printed for it.

! [*shell_command*]
> Shell escape. With no command specified, runs a Unix shell. If a command is specified, runs the command in a Unix shell.

altname *filename*
> Causes *smbclient* to request from the server and then print the old-style, 8.3-format filename for the specified file.

---

cancel *print_jobid* [...]
> Causes *smbclient* to request the server to cancel one or more print jobs, as specified by the numeric job IDs provided as arguments. See also the *queue* command, which prints job IDs.

chmod *filename octal_mode*
> Requests that the server change the Unix file permissions on *filename* to *octal_mode*, specified in octal numeric format. Works only if the server supports Unix CIFS extensions.

chown *filename UID GID*
> Requests that the server change the owner and group of the file specified by *filename* to those provided as decimal numeric arguments *UID* and *GID*. Works only if the server supports Unix CIFS extensions.

cd *[directory]*
> With no argument, prints the current working directory on the remote system. If a directory name is supplied as an argument, changes the working directory on the remote system to that specified.

del *filename*
> Requests that the server delete one or more files, as specified by the argument, from the current working directory. The argument can be a filename globbing pattern using the * and ? characters.

dir *[filename]*
> With no arguments, prints a list of files and directories in the working directory on the server. If an argument is provided, only files and directories whose names match the argument will be listed. The argument can be a filename globbing pattern using the * and ? characters.

exit
> Quits the *smbclient* program after terminating the SMB connection to the server.

get *remote_file [local_file]*
> Copies the file specified by *remote_file* from the server to the local system. If no *local_file* argument is specified, *smbclient* will name the local file same as it is named on the server. If *local_file* is specified, it will be used as the name of the local copy. See also the *lowercase* command.

---

help *[command]*
> A synonym for the *?* command.

lcd *[directory]*
> If no argument is provided, prints the name of *smbclient*'s working directory on the local system. If a directory name is provided as an argument, changes *smbclient*'s working directory to the directory specified.

link *link_name filename*
> Requests that the server create a hard link to *filename* and name it *link_name*. This command works only if the server supports Unix CIFS extensions.

lowercase
> Toggles the boolean lowercasing setting. When this setting is on, names of files copied from the server with the *get* and *mget* commands will be changed to all lowercase. This is mainly used for accessing servers that report filenames in all uppercase only.

ls *[filename]*
> A synonym for *dir*.

mask *[globbing_pattern]*
> Sets the filename globbing pattern for use with the *mget* and *mput* commands when recursion is turned on. (When recursion is off, the setting has no effect.) Both *mget* and *mput* accept a globbing pattern as arguments; however, those patterns apply only to the current directory. This command specifies the pattern used for all subdirectories that are recursively traversed. The pattern stays in effect until it is changed with another *mask* command. To return the setting to its original default, specify a *globbing_pattern* of an asterisk (*), which matches all files. See also the *mget*, *mput*, and *recurse* commands.

mdir *directory*
> A synonym for the *mkdir* command.

mget *pattern*
> When recursion is turned off, copies files matching the file-globbing pattern, as specified by the argument, from the current working directory on the server to the local system. When recursion is on, the *pattern* argument is used to match directories in the current working directory, and the pattern

specified by the *mask* command is used for matching files within each directory and all subdirectories. See also the *lowercase*, *mask*, and *recurse* commands.

print *filename*
> Prints the specified file. This requires that *smbclient* be connected to a print share. See also the *printmode* command.

printmode *mode*
> Sets the mode that is used by the *print* command. The mode can be either text, for printing text files such as the ASCII files commonly found on Unix, or graphics, for printing binary files.

prompt
> Toggles the prompting mode. When prompting is on (the default), the *mget* and *mput* commands will interactively prompt the user for permission to transfer each file. The user can answer either y (yes) or n (no), followed by a newline, to this prompt. When prompting is off, all the files will be transferred with no prompts issued.

put *local_file [remote_file]*
> Copies the file specified by *local_file* from the local to the remote system. If no *remote_file* argument is specified, *smbclient* will name the remote file the same as it is named on the local system. If *remote_file* is specified, it will be used as the name of the remote copy. See also the *lowercase* command.

queue
> Prints information on the print queue on the server. This requires that *smbclient* is connected to a print share.

quit
> A synonym for *exit*.

rd *directory*
> A synonym for *rmdir*.

recurse
> Toggles the recursion mode, which affects the *mget* and *mput* commands. When recursion is off (the default), the *mget* and *mput* commands will copy only files from the current working directory that match the file-globbing pattern specified as an argument to the command, and the pattern set by the *mask* command is ignored. When recursion is turned on, the *mget*

and *mput* commands recursively traverse any directories that match the pattern specified as the argument to the command, and the pattern set by the *mask* command is used to match files in those directories.

rm *filename*

A synonym for *del*.

rmdir *directory*

Requests that the server remove the specified directory.

setmode *filename attributes*

Requests that the server assign the specified MS-DOS file attributes on the specified file. The *attributes* argument has the format of a leading plus sign (+) or minus sign (-) either to set or to unset the attribute(s), respectively, followed by one or more of the characters r (read), s (system), h (hidden), or a (archive).

symlink *link_name filename*

Requests that the server create a symbolic link named *link_name* to *filename*. This command works only if the server supports Unix CIFS extensions. The server will not create a link that refers to a file not in the share to which *smbclient* is connected.

tar *cmd_str*

Performs an archiving operation using the tar format. This is the interactive form of the -T command-line operation, and the *cmd_str* argument is specified in the same manner. See also the *tarmode* command.

blocksize *size*

Sets the block size, in units of 512 bytes, for files written by the *tar* command.

tarmode *mode* ...

Specifies how the *tar* command performs its archiving, including how it handles the archive attribute on files. Multiple *mode* arguments can be provided, chosen from the following:

full

All files will be included, regardless of whether their archive attribute is set. This is the default.

inc
> Only files that have the `archive` attribute set will be included in the backup.

reset
> The `archive` attribute will be unset by *tar* after the file is included in the archive.

noreset
> The `archive` attribute will be left unchanged. This is the default.

system
> Files with the `system` attribute set will be included in the archive. This is the default.

nosystem
> Files with the `system` attribute set will not be included in the archive.

hidden
> Files with the `hidden` attribute set will be included in the archive. This is the default.

nohidden
> Files with the `hidden` attribute set will not be included in the archive.

verbose
> As files are included in the archive (when creating the archive) or are read from the archive (when extracting it), the name of each file will be printed. This is the default.

noverbose
> This turns verbose mode off, causing *tar* to perform its work quietly.

quiet
> An antonym for the `verbose` mode. When quiet is on, verbose is off, and vice versa.

---

smbcontrol

```
smbcontrol -i [options]
smbcontrol [options] process message-type [parameters]
```

The *smbcontrol* command sends control messages to running *smbd* or *nmbd* processes.

Options

-i
> Runs *smbcontrol* interactively, executing commands until a blank line or "q" is read. The user must have superuser privileges.

-s *filename*
> Specifies the location of the Samba configuration file.

-d *debuglevel*
> Sets the debugging level for logging. The debug level can be set from 0 to 10.

Whether *smbcontrol* commands are issued in interactive mode or from the command line, the commands are in the same format. Each command has up to three parts:

process
> Specifies the process or group of processes to which to send the message. If *process* is smbd, all *smbd* processes will receive the message. If *process* is nmbd, only the main *nmbd* process (identified by Samba's *nmbd.pid* file) receives the message. If *process* is the numeric PID of a running process on the system, that process will receive the message.

message-type
> Specifies the type of message that is sent. For more information, see "smbcontrol message types."

parameters
> Specifies additional parameters required by some messages.

smbcontrol message types

close-share *share_name*
> Closes the connection to a share or shares. If *share_name* is specified as an asterisk (*), connections to all shares will be closed. To close a single connection, *share_name* is given as the name of a share, as specified in the Samba configuration file, not including the enclosing brackets. Warning: no message is printed if there is an error in specifying *share_name*.

debug *num*
> Sets the debugging level. The *num* parameter specifies the level, which can be from 0 to 10.

debuglevel
> Prints the current debugging level.

force-election
> Can be used only with *nmbd*, telling it to force a master browser election.

ping *number*
> Sends *number* of pings and reports when they receive a reply or timeout. Used for connectivity testing.

profile *mode*
> Controls profiling statistics collection. If *mode* is on, profile statistics will be collected. If *mode* is off, collection of statistics is turned off. If *mode* is specified as count, only counting statistics are collected (and not timing statistics). If *mode* is flush, the data set is cleared (initialized).

profilelevel
> Prints the current profiling level.

printer-notify *printer_name*
> Sends a printer notify message to Windows NT/2000/XP for the specified printer. This message can be sent only to *smbd*. Warning: no message is printed if the *printer_name* parameter is specified incorrectly.

---

smbgroupedit

smbgroupedit *[options]*

This command, new to Samba 3.0, sets up mappings between Unix groups and Windows NT/2000/XP groups and also allows a Unix group to become a domain group. This command must be run by the superuser.

Options

-a *Unix_group_name*
> Adds a mapping for the specified Unix group. The -n option is used along with this option to specify the Windows NT group to which the Unix group is mapped.

-c *SID*
> Changes a mapping between a Windows NT group and a Unix group. The Windows NT group is specified as a SID with this option, and the Unix group is specified with the -u option.

-d *description*

Specifies a comment for the mapping, which will be stored along with it.

-l

When used with the -v option, prints a long listing. This is the default. The information printed includes the name of the Windows NT group, its SID, its corresponding Unix group (if a mapping has been defined), the group type, the comment, and the privileges of the group.

-n *Windows_group_name*

Specifies the name of the Windows NT group. Used with the -a option.

-p *privilege*

Used along with the -a option to specify a Windows NT privilege to be given to the Unix group.

-s

When used with the -v option, prints a short listing. The information printed includes just the name of the Windows NT group, its SID, and, if a mapping has been defined, its corresponding Unix group. This option is useful for determining the SID of a group, for use with the -c option.

-t *TYPE*

Assigns a Windows group type to the group. *TYPE* is a single character, and is one of b (built-in), d (domain), or l (local).

-u *Unix_group_name*

Specifies the name of the Unix group to map to the Windows NT group. Used with the -c option.

-v

Prints a list of groups in the Windows NT domain in which the Samba server is operating. See also the -l and -s options.

-x *Unix_group_name*

Deletes the mapping for the Unix group specified.

smbmnt

smbmnt mnt_point [*options*]

This is a low-level helper program for mounting smbfs filesystems. It used by *smbmount* to do the privileged part of the mount operation on behalf of an ordinary user. Generally, users should not run this command directly.

Options

-r

    Mounts the filesystem as read-only.

-u *uid*

    Specifies the UID to use for the owner of the files.

-g *gid*

    Specifies the GID to use for the group of the files.

-f *mask*

    Specifies the octal file mask.

-d *mask*

    Specifies the octal directory mask.

-o *options*

    Specifies the list of options that are passed to the smbfs module.

To allow users to mount SMB shares without help from an administrator, set the "set user ID" permission on the *smbmnt* executable. However, note that this can raise security issues.

---

smbmount

smbmount *service mount_point* [*-o options*]

This program mounts an smbfs filesystem on a mount point in the Unix filesystem. It is typically called as *mount.smb* from *mount*, although it can also be run directly by users. After mounting the smbfs filesystem, *smbmount* continues to run as a daemon as long as the filesystem is mounted. It logs events in the file *log.smbmount* in the same directory as the other Samba log files (which is commonly */usr/local/samba/var* by default). The logging level is controlled by the debug level parameter in the Samba configuration file.

The service argument specifies the SMB share to mount, given as a UNC. The *mount_point* argument specifies a directory to use as the mount point. The options to *smbmount* are specified as a comma-separated list of *key=value* pairs. The documented options are as follows. Others can be passed if the kernel supports them.

Options

username=*name*

> Specifies the username to connect as. If this is not provided, the environment variable USER will be tried. The name can be specified as *username%password*, *user/workgroup*, or *user/workgroup%password*.

password=*string*

> Specifies the SMB password. If no password is provided using this option, the *username* option, or the *credentials* option, the environment variable PASSWD is used. If that also does not exist, *smbmount* will prompt interactively for a password.

credentials=*filename*

> Specifies a file that contains a username and password in the following format:

        username = *value*
        password = *value*

uid=*number*

> Sets the Unix user ID to be used as the owner of all files in the mounted filesystem. It can be specified as a username or numeric UID. Defaults to the UID of the user running *smbmount*.

gid=*number*

> Sets the Unix group ID to be used as the group for all files in the mounted filesystem. It can be specified as a group name or a numeric GID. Defaults to the GID of the user running *smbmount*.

port=*number*

> Sets the TCP port number. This is 139, which is required by most Windows versions.

fmask=*octal_mask*

> Sets the Unix permissions of all files in the mounted filesystem. Defaults to the user's current umask.

dmask=*octal_mask*

> Sets the Unix permissions of all directories in the mounted filesystem. Defaults to the current umask.

debug=*number*

> Sets the debugging level.

ip=*host*
>   Sets the destination hostname or IP address.

netbiosname=*name*
>   Sets the computer name to connect as. This defaults to the hostname of the local system.

workgroup=*name*
>   Sets the workgroup or domain.

sockopt=*opts*
>   Sets TCP socket options.

scope=*num*
>   Sets the NetBIOS scope.

guest
>   Don't expect or prompt for a password.

ro
>   Mounts the share read-only.

rw
>   Mounts the share read-write.

iocharset=*charset*
>   Sets the charset used by the Linux machine for codepage-to-charset translation. See also the *codepage* option.

codepage=*page*
>   Sets the DOS code page. See also the *iocharset* option.

ttl=*milliseconds*
>   Sets the time to live, in milliseconds, for entries in the directory cache. A higher value gives better performance on large directories and/or slower connections. The default is 1000ms. Try 10000ms (10 seconds) as a starting value if directory operations are visibly slow.

smbpasswd

smbpasswd *[options] [username] [password]*
smbpasswd *[options] [password]*

The *smbpasswd* program provides the general function of managing encrypted passwords. How it works depends on whether it is run by the superuser or an ordinary user.

For the superuser, *smbpasswd* can be used to maintain Samba's *smbpasswd* file. It can add or delete users, change their passwords, and modify other attributes pertaining to the user that are held in the *smbpasswd* file.

When run by ordinary users, *smbpasswd* can be used only to change their encrypted passwords. In this mode of operation, *smbpasswd* acts as a client to the *smbd* daemon. The program will fail if *smbd* is not operating, if the hosts allow or hosts deny parameters in the Samba configuration file do not permit connections from localhost (IP address 127.0.0.1), or if the encrypted passwords option is set to no. It is also possible for *smbpasswd* to change a user's password when it is maintained on a remote system, including a Windows NT domain controller.

Superuser-only options

-a *username*

> Adds a user to the encrypted password file. The user must already exist in the system password file (*/etc/passwd*). If the user already exists in the *smbpasswd* file, the -a option changes the existing password.

-d *username*

> Disables a user in the encrypted password file. The user's entry in the file will remain, but will be marked with a flag disabling the user from authenticating.

-e *username*

> Enables a disabled user in the encrypted password file. This overrides the effect of the -d option.

-j *domain*

> Joins the Samba server to a Windows NT domain as a domain member server. The *domain* argument is the NetBIOS name of the Windows NT domain that is being joined. See also the -r and -U options.

-m

> Indicates that the account is a computer account in a Windows NT domain rather than a domain user account.

-n

> Sets the user's password to a null password. For the user to authenticate, the parameter null passwords = yes must exist in the [global] section of the Samba configuration file.

-R *resolve_order_list*

Sets the resolve order of the name servers. This option is similar to the resolve order configuration option and can take any of the four parameters lmhosts, host, wins, and bcast, in any order. If more than one is specified, the argument is specified as a space-separated list.

-w *password*

Used when Samba has been compiled with the --with-ldapsam configure option. Specifies the password that goes with the value of the ldap admin dn Samba configuration file parameter.

-x *username*

Deletes the user from the *smbpasswd* file. This is a one-way operation, and all information associated with the entry is lost. To disable the account without deleting the user's entry in the file, see the -d option.

Other options

-c *filename*

Specifies the Samba configuration file, overriding the compiled-in default.

-D *debug_level*

Sets the debug (also called logging) level. The level can range from 0 to 10. Debug level 0 logs only the most important messages; level 1 is normal; levels 3 and above are primarily for debugging and slow the program considerably.

-h

Prints command-line usage information.

-L

Causes *smbpasswd* to run in local mode, in which ordinary users are allowed to use the superuser-only options. This requires that the *smbpasswd* file be made readable and writable by the user. This is for testing purposes.

-r *NetBIOS_name*

Specifies on which machine the password should change. If changing a Windows NT domain password, the remote system specified by *NetBIOS_name* must be the PDC for the domain. The user's username on the local system is used by default. See also the -U option for use when the user's Samba username is different from the local username.

`-R resolve_order`

> Sets the resolve order of the name servers. This option is similar to the resolve order configuration option and can take any of the four parameters lmhosts, host, wins, and bcast, in any order. If more than one is specified, the argument is specified as a space-separated list.

`-s username`

> Causes *smbpasswd* not to prompt for passwords from */dev/tty*, but instead to read the old and new passwords from the standard input. This is useful when calling *smbpasswd* from a script.

`-S`

> Queries the domain controller of the domain, as specified by the workgroup parameter in the Samba configuration file, and retrieves the domain's SID. This will then be used as the SID for the local system. A specific PDC can be selected by combining this option with the -r option, and its domain's SID will be used. This option is for migrating domain accounts from a Windows NT primary domain controller to a Samba PDC.

`-U username[%password]`

> Changes the password for *username* on the remote system. This is to handle instances in which the remote username and local username are different. This option requires that -r also be used. Often used with -j to provide the username of the administrative user on the primary domain controller for adding computer accounts.

smbsh

The *smbsh* program allows SMB shares to be accessed from a Unix system. When *smbsh* is run, an extra directory tree called */smb* becomes available to dynamically linked shell commands. The first level of directories under */smb* represent available workgroups, the next level of subdirectories represent the SMB servers in each workgroup, and the third level of subdirectories represent the disk and printer shares of each server.

Samba must be compiled with the `--with-smbwrappers` option to enable *smbsh*.

Options

-d *debug_level*

Sets the debug (sometimes called logging) level. The level can range from 0, the default, to 10. Debug level 0 logs only the most important messages; level 1 is normal; levels 3 and above are primarily for debugging and slow *smbsh* considerably.

-l *filename*

Sets the name of the logging file. By default, messages are sent to *stderr*.

-L *directory*

Specifies the location of *smbsh*'s shared libraries, overriding the compiled-in default.

-P *prefix*

Sets the name of the root directory to use for the SMB filesystem. The default is */smb*.

-R *resolve_order*

Sets the resolve order of the name servers. This option is similar to the resolve order configuration option and can take any of the four parameters lmhosts, host, wins, and bcast, in any order. If more than one is specified, the argument is specified as a space-separated list.

-U *username*

Provides the username, and optionally the password, for authenticating the connection to the SMB server. The password can be supplied using the *username%password* format. If either or both the username and password are not provided, *smbsh* will prompt interactively for them.

-W *workgroup*

Specifies the NetBIOS workgroup or domain to which the client will connect. This overrides the workgroup parameter in the Samba configuration file and is sometimes necessary to connect to some servers.

smbspool

smbspool *job user title copies options filename*

The *smbspool* program provides a CUPS-compatible interface to Samba printing by providing a way to send a print job to an SMB printer using the command-line format specified by CUPS printers. Although *smbspool* is designed to work best with CUPS printers, it can be used to send print jobs to non-CUPS Samba printers as well.

The arguments for *smbspool*, as shown here, are those used in the CUPS printing system. However, some of the arguments are currently ignored because they don't correspond to the Samba printing system. These arguments must be supplied in the command and can be filled in with "dummy" values.

The *job* argument refers to the job number and is currently ignored. The *user* argument is the name of the user who submitted the print job and is also ignored. The *title* argument is the name of the print job and must be supplied. It is used as the name of the remote print file. The *copies* argument is the number of copies that will be printed. This number is used only if the (optional) *filename* argument is supplied. Otherwise, only one copy is printed. The *options* argument (used to specify printing options), is ignored. The *filename* argument is used for specifying the name of the file to be printed. If it is not provided, the standard input will be used.

The printer that the job is to be sent to is specified in the DEVICE_URI environment variable. The format for the printer name is a device Universal Resource Indicator, which can be in any of the following formats:

```
smb://server/printer
smb://workgroup/server/printer
smb://username:password@server/printer
smb://username:password@workgroup/server/printer
```

smbstatus

This program lists the current connections on a Samba server.

Options

-b

> Causes *smbstatus* to produce brief output. This includes the version of Samba and auditing information about the users that are connected to the server.

-d

> Gives verbose output, which includes a list of services, a list of locked files, and memory usage statistics. This is the default.

-L

  Prints only the list of current file locks.

-p

  Prints only a list of *smbd* process IDs.

-P

  Prints only the contents of the profiling memory area. Requires that Samba has been compiled with the profiling option.

-S

  Prints only a list of shares and their connections.

-s *filename*

  Specifies the Samba configuration file to use when processing this command.

-u *username*

  Limits the report to the activity of a single user.

---

smbtar

smbtar *[options]*

The *smbtar* program is a shell-script wrapper around *smbclient* for doing tar-format archiving operations. It is functionally very similar to the Unix *tar* program.

Options

-a

  Resets (clears) the archive attribute on files after they are backed up. The default is to leave the archive attribute unchanged.

-b *blocksize*

  Sets block size, in units of 512 bytes, for reading or writing the archive file. Defaults to 20, which results in a block size of 10240 bytes.

-d *directory*

  Changes the working directory on the remote system to *directory* before starting the restore or backup operation.

-i

  Specifies incremental mode; files are backed up only if they have the DOS archive attribute set. The archive attribute is reset (cleared) after each file is read.

-l *log_level*

    Sets the logging level. This corresponds to the -d option of *smbclient* and other Samba programs.

-N *filename*

    Backs up only files newer than *filename*. For incremental backups.

-p *password*

    Specifies the password to use to access a share. An alternative to using the *username%password* format with the -u option.

-r

    Restores files to the share from the tar file.

-s *server*

    Specifies the SMB server. See also the -x option.

-t *filename*

    Specifies the file or Unix device to use as the archiving medium. The default is *tar.out* or the value of the TAPE environment variable, if it has been set.

-u *username*

    Specifies the user account to use when connecting to the share. You can specify the password as well, in the format *username%password*. The username defaults to the user's Unix username.

-v

    Operates in verbose mode, printing error messages and additional information that can be used in debugging and monitoring. Backup and restore operations will list each file as it is processed.

-x *share*

    States the name of the share on the server to which to connect. The default is backup. See also the -s option.

-X *file_list*

    Tells *smbtar* to exclude the specified files from the backup or restore operation.

smbumount

smbumount *mount_point*

The *smbumount* command exists to allow an ordinary (nonsupe-ruser) user to unmount a smbfs filesystem, which the user had previously mounted using *smbmount*.

For ordinary users to issue the command, *smbumount* must be made suid root.

testparm

testparm *[options] [filename] [hostname IP_addr]*

The *testparm* program checks a Samba configuration file for obvious errors.

If the configuration file is not provided using the *filename* argument, then it defaults to */usr/local/samba/lib/smb.conf*. If the hostname and an IP address of a system are included, an extra check is made to ensure that the system is allowed to connect to each service defined in the configuration file. This is done by comparing the hostname and IP address to the definitions of the hosts allow and hosts deny parameters.

Options

-h

>   Prints usage information for the program.

-L *server_name*

>   Sets the %L configuration variable to the specified server name.

-s

>   Disables the default behavior of prompting for the Enter key to be pressed before printing the list of configuration options for the server.

testprns

testprns *printername [printcapname]*

This is a very simple program that checks to see if a specified printer name exists in the system printer capabilities (printcap) file.

If *printcapname* isn't specified, Samba attempts to use the one specified in the Samba configuration file with the `printcap name` parameter. If none is specified there, Samba will try */etc/printcap*.

wbinfo

`wbinfo [options]`

This program retrieves and prints information from the *winbindd* daemon, which must be running for *wbinfo* to function.

Options

`-u`

Prints all usernames that have been mapped from the Windows NT domain to Unix users. Users in all trusted domains are also listed.

`-g`

Prints all group names that have been mapped from the Windows NT domain to Unix groups. Groups in all trusted domains are also reported.

`-h NetBIOS_name`

Queries the WINS server and prints the IP address of the specified system.

`-n name`

Prints the SID corresponding to the name specified. The argument can be specified as *DOMAIN/name* (or by using a character other than the slash, as defined by the winbind separator character) to specify both the domain and the name. If the domain and separator are omitted, the value of the `workgroup` parameter in the Samba configuration file is used as the name of the domain.

`-s SID`

Prints the name mapped to a SID, which is specified in the format `S-1-N-N-D-D-D-R`.

`-U UID`

Prints the SID mapped to a Unix UID, if one exists in the current domain.

`-G gid`

Prints the SID mapped to a Unix group ID, if one exists in the current domain.

-S *SID*

> Prints the Unix UID that winbind has mapped to the specified SID, if one exists.

-Y *SID*

> Prints the Unix group ID that winbind has mapped to the specified SID, if one exists.

-t

> Tests to see that the workstation trust account for the Samba server is valid.

-m

> Prints a list of Windows NT domains trusted by the Windows server. This does not include the PDC's domain.

-r *username*

> Prints the list of Unix group IDs to which the user belongs. This works only if the user's account is maintained on a domain controller.

-a *username%password*

> Checks to see if a user can authenticate through *winbindd* using the specified username and password.

-A *username%password*

> Saves the username and password used by *winbindd* to the domain controller. For use when operating in a Windows 2000 domain.

Example Configuration Files

In this section we provide examples of complete configuration files for running Samba in the various environments. Using one of these examples, you can run Samba as a workgroup authentication server, workgroup server, primary domain controller, or domain member server.

We have kept the examples simple so that they have the most universal application. If you need to get a Samba server up and running with minimal delay, use these examples as starting templates and modify them to fit your own needs. The comments inside the files indicate what needs to be changed, and how, to work on a particular system on your network.

Samba in a Workgroup

If your network is configured as a workgroup, adding a Samba server is pretty simple. Samba even lets you add features (such as user-level security and WINS) that would normally require an expensive Windows NT/2000 Server.

Authentication and WINS server

In a workgroup environment, Samba can be set up with share-level security and without offering WINS name service. This works and is simple, but we generally recommend that user-level security be enabled to allow Windows 95/98/Me systems to make use of it. Also, it only takes a single parameter to enable Samba as a WINS server, resulting in far better network efficiency. Here is the configuration file that does it:

```
[global]
    # replace "toltec" with your system's hostname

    netbios name = toltec

    # replace "METRAN" with the name of your workgroup

    workgroup = METRAN

    security = user
    encrypt passwords = yes

    # Run a WINS server

    wins support = yes

    # The following three lines ensure that the Samba
    # server will maintain the role of master browser.
    # Make sure no other Samba server has its OS level
    # set higher than it is here.

    local master = yes
    preferred master = yes
    os level = 65

    # Make home directories on the server available to users.
```

```
[homes]
    comment = %u's Home Directory
    browsable = no
    read only = no
    map archive = yes

# This is a shared directory, accessible by all
# users. Use your own share name and path.

[d]
    path = /d
    create mask = 0700
    read only = no
```

Generally, you will use a configuration file similar to this one when adding your first Samba server to the workgroup.

Workgroup server

Things are a little different if another system—either a Samba server or Windows NT/2000 server—is already running as a WINS server. In this case, Samba is configured to use that server for NetBIOS name resolution. Here is a configuration file that does this:

```
[global]
    # replace "mixtec" with your system's hostname

    netbios name = mixtec

    # replace "METRAN" with your workgroup name

    workgroup = METRAN

    security = user
    encrypt passwords = yes

    # Replace "172.16.1.1" with the IP address
    # of your WINS server. If there is none,
    # omit this line.

    wins server = 172.16.1.1

    # The OS level is set to 17 to allow
    # this system to win over all Windows
```

```
      # versions, but not the Samba server
      # that uses the configuration file
      # in the previous section.

      os level = 17

[homes]
      comment = %u's Home Directory
      browsable = no
      read only = no

# This is a shared directory, accessible by all
# users. Use your own share name and path.

[d]
      path = /d
      create mask = 0700
      read only = no
```

Once you have a server in your workgroup handling authentication and WINS, this is the configuration file to use when adding additional Samba servers to the workgroup.

Samba in a Windows NT Domain

When operating in a Windows NT domain, Samba can act either as a primary domain controller or as a domain member server.

Primary domain controller

Setting up Samba as a primary domain controller is more complicated than the other configurations. However, the extra difficulty is offset by having a more secure network and additional features such as logon scripts and roaming profiles. In the following configuration file, we also include support for a Microsoft Dfs share:

```
[global]
      # Replace "toltec" with the hostname of your system.

      netbios name = toltec
```

```
# Replace "METRAN" with the name
# of your Windows NT domain.

workgroup = METRAN

# Run a WINS server

wins support = yes

# Always act as the local master browser
# and domain master browser.  Do not allow
# any other system to take over these roles!

domain master = yes
local master = yes
preferred master = yes
os level = 255

# Perform domain authentication.

security = user
encrypt passwords = yes
domain logons = yes

# The location of user profiles
# for Windows NT/2000/XP.

logon path = \\%L\profiles\%u\%m

# Users' Windows home directories and storage of
# Win95/98/Me roaming profiles.

logon drive = G:
logon home = \\toltec\%u\.win_profile\%m

# The following line is optional because
# Samba always offers NetBIOS time service.
# This causes it to also be advertised:

time server = yes

# The logon script used for all users,
# Relative to [netlogon] share directory.

logon script = logon.bat
```

```
    # The group identifying administrative users.
    # If you have domain users in the Domain Admins
    # group, use them here instead of "jay".

    domain admin group = root jay

    # For adding machine accounts automatically.
    # This example works on Linux. For other host
    # operating systems, you might need a different
    # command.

    add user script = /usr/sbin/useradd -d \
      /dev/null -g 100 -s /bin/false -M %u

    # Provide Microsoft Dfs support.

    host msdfs = yes

# The netlogon share is required for
# functioning as the primary domain controller.
# Make sure the directory used for the path exists.

[netlogon]
    path = /usr/local/samba/lib/netlogon
    writable = no
    browsable = no

# The profiles share is for storing
# Windows NT/2000/XP roaming profiles.
# Use your own path, and make sure
# the directory exists.

[profiles]
    path = /home/samba-ntprof
    writable = yes
    create mask = 0600
    directory mask = 0700
    browsable = no

[homes]
    comment = Home Directory
    browsable = no
    read only = no
    map archive = yes
```

```
# The Dfs share.
# Use your own path, making
# sure the directory exists.

[dfs]
    comment = Dfs share
    path = /usr/local/samba/dfs
    msdfs root = yes

# A shared directory, accessible by all domain users.
# Use your own share name and path.

[d]
    comment = %u's Home Directory
    path = /d
    create mask = 0700
    read only = no
```

Domain member server

In a domain that already has either a Samba PDC or Windows NT/2000 Server PDC, additional Samba servers can be added as domain member servers using the following configuration file:

```
[global]
    # Replace "mixtec" with the system's hostname.

    netbios name = mixtec

    # Replace "METRAN" with the name of your domain.

    workgroup = METRAN

    # Replace "172.16.1.1" with the
    # IP address of your WINS server.

    wins server = 172.16.1.1

    os level = 33

    security = domain
    encrypt passwords = yes
    password server = *
```

```
# Home directories.

[homes]
    comment = %u's Home Directory
    browsable = no
    read only = no
    map archive = yes

# This is an example printers
# share, which works for Linux.

[printers]
    printable = yes
    printing = BSD
    print command = /usr/bin/lpr -P%p %s
    path = /var/tmp
    min print space = 2000

# A shared directory, accessible by all domain users.
# Use your own share name and path.

[d]
    path = /d
    create mask = 0755
    read only = no
```

Index

We'd like to hear your suggestions for improving our indexes. Send email to
index@oreilly.com.

Other Titles Available from O'Reilly

Linux

Using Samba, 2nd Edition

*By Jay Ts, Robert Eckstein &
David Collier-Brown
2nd Edition February 2003
450 pages, ISBN 0-596-00256-4*

The second edition of *Using Samba*
thoroughly covers configuration of
the new Samba versions, including
the SWAT graphical configuration
tool. The book also explores Samba's
new role as a secondary domain
controller, its support for the use of
Windows 2000 security on the host
Unix system, and Samba's better
integration with SSL security. Every-
thing is here, from basic installation
and configuration to advanced topics
in security, trouble-shooting, and
special environments.

Managing & Using MySQL, 2nd Edition

*By George Reese, Randy Jay Yarger &
Tim King
2nd Edition April 2002
448 pages, ISBN 0-596-00211-4*

This edition retains the best features
of the first edition, while adding the
latest on MySQL and the relevant
programming language interfaces, with
more complete reference information.
The administration section is greatly
enhanced; the programming language
chapters have been updated—especially the Perl and PHP chapters—
and new additions include chapters
on security and extending MySQL
and a system tables reference.

Linux Network Administrator's Guide, 2nd Edition

*By Olaf Kirch & Terry Dawson
2nd Edition June 2000
506 pages, ISBN 1-56592-400-2*

Fully updated, this comprehensive,
impressive introduction to networking on Linux now covers firewalls,
including the use of ipchains and
iptables (netfilter), masquerading,
and accounting. Other new topics
include Novell (NCP/IPX) support
and INN (news administration).
Original material on serial connections, UUCP, routing and DNS, mail
and News, SLIP and PPP, NFS, and
NIS has been thoroughly updated.

Understanding the Linux Kernel, 2nd Edition

*By Daniel P. Bovet & Marco Cesati
2nd Edition December 2002
784 pages, ISBN 0-596-00213-0*

Understanding the Linux Kernel helps
readers understand how Linux performs best and how it meets the
challenge of different environments.
The authors introduce each topic by
explaining its importance, and show
how kernel operations relate to the
utilities that are familiar to Unix
programmers and users. This popu-
lar book provides a guided tour of
the code that forms the core of all
Linux operating systems. It also
explains the theoretical underpin-
nings for why Linux (and many
other operating systems) do things
the way they do.

O'REILLY®

To order: *800-998-9938* • *order@oreilly.com* • *www.oreilly.com*
Online editions of most O'Reilly titles are available by subscription at *safari.oreilly.com*
Also available at most retail and online bookstores.

Unix Power Tools, 3rd Edition

By Shelley Powers, Jerry Peek, Tim
O'Reilly & Mike Loukides
3rd Edition October 2002
1156 pages, ISBN 0-596-00330-7

In addition to vital information on Linux, Darwin and BSD, *Unix Power Tools*, 3rd Edition now offers more coverage of bash, zsh and other new shells, along with discussions on modern utilities and applications. Several sections focus on security and Internet access, acknowledging that most Unix boxes are connected to the Internet. And there is a new chapter on access to Unix from Windows, addressing the heterogeneous nature of systems today.

Linux Device Drivers, 2nd Edition

By Alessandro Rubini &
Jonathan Corbet
2nd Edition June 2001
586 pages, ISBN 0-59600-008-1

This practical guide is for anyone who wants to support computer peripherals under the Linux operating system. It shows step-by-step how to write a driver for character devices, block devices, and network interfaces, illustrating with examples you can compile and run. The second edition covers Kernel 2.4 and adds discussions of symmetric multiprocessing (SMP), Universal Serial Bus (USB), and some new platforms.

Linux Security Cookbook

By Daniel J. Barrett, Richard Silverman
& Robert G. Byrnes
1st Edition June 2003 (est.)
352 pages (est.), ISBN 0-569-00391-9

The *Linux Security Cookbook* includes a series of easy-to-follow recipes—short, focused pieces of code that administrators can use to improve security and perform common tasks securely. This guide includes real solutions to a wide range of targeted problems, such as sending encrypted email within Emacs, restricting access to network services at particular times of day, firewalling a webserver, preventing IP spoofing, setting up key-based SSH authentication, and much more. The *Linux Security Cookbook* gives administrators a way to close common security holes quickly without having to look up specific syntax.

Essential CVS

By Jennifer Vesperman
1st Edition June 2003 (est.)
400 pages (est.), ISBN 0-596-00459-1

Essential CVS is a complete and easy-to-follow reference that helps programmers and system administrators bring order to the task of managing large quantities of documents. The book covers basic concepts and usage of CVS, and features a comprehensive reference for CVS commandsincluding a handy Command Reference Card for quick on-the-job checks.

Building Secure Servers with Linux

By Michael D. Bauer
1st Edition October 2002
448 pages, 0-596-00217-3

This book provides a unique balance of "big picture" principles that transcend specific software packages and version numbers, and very clear procedures on securing some of those software packages. An all-inclusive resource for Linux users who wish to harden their systems, the book covers general security as well as key services such as DNS, the Apache Web server, mail, file transfer, and secure shell.

Linux Server Hacks

By Rob Flickenger
1st Edition January 2003
240 pages, 0-596-00461-3

Linux Server Hacks is a collection of 100 industrial-strength hacks, providing tips and tools that solve practical problems for Linux system administrators. Every hack can be read in just a few minutes but will save hours of searching for the right answer. Some of the hacks are subtle, many of them are non-obvious, and all of them demonstrate the power and flexibility of a Linux system. *Linux Server Hacks* also helps you manage large-scale Web installations running Apache, MySQL, and other open source tools that are typically part of a Linux system.

Extreme Programming Pocket Guide

By chromatic
1st Edition June 2003 (est.)
80 pages (est.), ISBN 0-596-00485-0

This guide serves as a clear-cut introduction to Extreme Programming by summarizing the goals, rules, and general philosophy of XP in a short, concise manner. Programmers will quickly come up to speed on why and how they can effectively use this deliberate and disciplined approach to software development for large-scale business applications.

Unix Basics

Learning the UNIX Operating System, 5th Edition

By Jerry Peek, Grace Todino
& John Strang
5th Edition October 2001
176 pages, ISBN 0-596-00261-0

Learning the UNIX Operating System is the most effective introduction to Unix in print. The fifth edition covers Internet usage for email, file transfers, and web browsing. It's perfect for those who are just starting with Unix or Linux, as well as anyone who encounters a Unix system on the Internet. Complete with a quick-reference card to pull out and keep handy, it's an ideal primer for Mac and PC users of the Internet who need to know a little bit about Unix on the systems they visit.

O'REILLY®

To order: *800-998-9938* • *order@oreilly.com* • *www.oreilly.com*
Online editions of most O'Reilly titles are available by subscription at *safari.oreilly.com*
Also available at most retail and online bookstores.

Unix Basics

Learning the Korn Shell, 2nd Edition

By Bill Rosenblatt, Arnold Robbins
2nd Edition April 2002
432 pages, ISBN 0-596-00195-9

Learning the Korn Shell is the key to gaining control of the Korn shell and becoming adept at using it as an interactive command and scripting language. Readers will learn how to write many applications more easily and quickly than with other high-level languages. A solid offering for many years, this newly revised title inherits a long tradition of trust among computer professionals who want to learn or refine an essential skill.

UNIX in a Nutshell: System V Edition, 3rd Edition

By Arnold Robbins
3rd Edition September 1999
616 pages, ISBN 1-56592-427-4

The bestselling, most informative Unix reference book is now more complete and up-to-date. Not a scaled-down quick reference of common commands, *UNIX in a Nutshell* is a complete reference containing all commands and options, with descriptions and examples that put the commands in context. For all but the thorniest Unix problems, this one reference should be all you need. Covers System V Release 4 and Solaris 7.

Using csh and tcsh

By Paul DuBois
1st Edition August 1995
242 pages, ISBN 1-56592-132-1

Using csh and tcsh describes from the beginning how to use these shells interactively to get your work done faster with less typing. You'll learn how to make your prompt tell you where you are (no more pwd); use what you've typed before (history); type long command lines with few keystrokes (command and filename completion); remind yourself of filenames when in the middle of typing a command; and edit a botched command without retyping it.

Learning GNU Emacs, 2nd Edition

By Debra Cameron, Bill Rosenblatt & Eric Raymond
2nd Edition September 1996
560 pages, ISBN 1-56592-152-6

Learning GNU Emacs is an introduction to Version 19.30 of the GNU Emacs editor, one of the most widely used and powerful editors available under Unix. It provides a solid introduction to basic editing, a look at several important "editing modes" (special Emacs features for editing specific types of documents, including email, Usenet News, and the World Wide Web), and a brief introduction to customization and Emacs LISP programming. The book is aimed at new Emacs users, whether or not they are programmers. Includes quick-reference card.

O'REILLY®

To order: *800-998-9938* • *order@oreilly.com* • *www.oreilly.com*
Online editions of most O'Reilly titles are available by subscription at *safari.oreilly.com*
Also available at most retail and online bookstores.